Think about it

Think
about it

IDEAS AND INSPIRATION

FOR TODAY'S HAWAI'I

JOHN FINK

WATERMARK
PUBLISHING

▲▲▲▲

ISBN 978-1-948011-25-9

Library of Congress Control Number: 2020931459

Think About It editorials used with permission of Gray Media Group, Inc.

Design and production
Kurt Osaki
Allie Kuritani
Osaki Creative Group

Cover photography
David Croxford

Watermark Publishing
1000 Bishop St., Ste. 806
Honolulu, HI 96813
Telephone 1-808-587-7766
Toll-free 1-866-900-BOOK
sales@bookshawaii.net
www.bookshawaii.net

Printed in Korea

Introduction

As I pored over the nearly 2,000 editorials that I wrote and aired for television from 2000 to 2019, one thing became readily apparent: the high number of important local issues that surfaced again and again—without much, if any, resolution. Homelessness, lack of air-conditioning in our kids' classrooms, inadequate parental responsibility in education, potholes, the Haʻiku Stairway to Heaven, the Waikiki Natatorium, Hawaiʻi's lack of economic diversity, the state of the aloha spirit, the loss of our uniqueness, holiday season-only good cheer, lethargic inaction by our elected officials, Hawaiʻi's anemic two-party system, the future of tourism… the list goes on and on, as many topics demanded attention again and again due to circumstantial changes over two decades.

Airing these editorials on television stations KHNL and KFVE (2000-2009) and then on KFVE alone (2009-2019) was actually a mandate from our corporate hierarchy. I was vice president and general manager at both stations, and Raycom Media (acquired by Gray TV at the beginning of 2019) believed strongly in community, and that its stations throughout the country should take editorial positions on key community issues. Raycom management stated that "it is the vision of the company that it be involved in the communities its broadcast properties serve." Raycom believed that editorials could further community dialog, an essential part of a local TV station's civic responsibility. This was a particular passion of Dr. David Bronner, the CEO of the Retirement Systems of Alabama (RSA). RSA was Raycom's lead lender, and Dr. Bronner watched and read station editorials from throughout Raycom's national TV empire. It was through the vision of Raycom Media CEO John Hayes and future CEO Paul McTear that Raycom came to buy KHNL and KFVE in mid-1999, and these "Think About It" editorials began in earnest early the following year. Messrs. Hayes and McTear, who had played integral roles on the management team of our former owner, the Providence Journal Company, encouraged RSA to buy our stations because Hayes and McTear loved Hawaiʻi and what it stands for. They also believed deeply in the KHNL/KFVE mantra of a dynamic management team committed to local programming, including sports and local news, as they had overseen KHNL/KFVE under the Providence Journal Company.

KHNL/KFVE represented numerous firsts in the broadcast industry, becoming America's first FCC-licensed duopoly (two stations owned in one market) on December 31, 1999, when KHNL bought KFVE after having a local market agreement for years. KHNL and KFVE also became the first all-digital newsroom in the world (yes, even before CNN) when the stations signed on with local news in mid-1995 in preparation for an upcoming network change, as KHNL switched from a FOX affiliate to an NBC affiliate on January 1, 1996. KHNL and then KFVE also boasted the most prolific television sports coverage of any university in the country, by way of its 28-year relationship with University of Hawai'i athletics (1984-2011). With an annual commitment to air many UH sports, including the so-called "minor" sports, KHNL and KFVE broadcast live more than 110 collegiate sporting events a year, sometimes airing as many as 125 events in a nine-month school year! For more than a quarter of a century, no other university in the country could claim to be as fully covered on TV as UH—which included promoting and pushing the growing women's sports of volleyball, basketball, soccer, water polo, and softball.

It was our savvy program director, Dan Schmidt, who coined the simple yet complete name for our editorial features: "Think About It." Dan understood that I wanted to share ideas, thoughts, suggestions, commentaries, and cautionary tales, most of which—about 80 percent of the time—reflected Hawai'i-specific themes, but sometimes ventured off into the broader realms of sociology, philosophy, spirituality, and my personal experiences. Two editorials aired twice weekly in or around local nightly newscasts, as the corporate folks wanted to ensure that these features ran in a quality time period with strong viewership. The idea was to engage and perhaps even challenge the audience.

One thing I'm most proud of is the fact that two editorials ran on KHNL and/or KFVE every single week for 19 years. We never missed one. When I was leaving town on a business trip or on vacation—or even in the hospital for surgery—I always taped enough editorials beforehand to ensure that new episodes aired twice a week, every week for almost two decades. (For you math majors, that's 104 editorials over 19 full years, or 1,976 editorials total.)

This book includes nearly 200 of them exactly as they aired— arguably we've cherry-picked the "best" editorials that might still resonate today, or were especially poignant when they first aired. Some of them have *footnotes in bold, italicized letters* that were added in January 2020 to indicate how far we've come—or not come, as the case may be—in the intervening years. All are in print here just as they aired on our TV stations, with no exceptions. Some themes might appear simply "local" at first, but the underlying idea is to connect the reader's mind and soul to show that everyone can truly make a difference while on planet Earth, be it individually or communally, at home, at work, or through charitable efforts.

These days, I'm happy to be back doing "Think About It" editorials, in print with a weekly column on page 2 in *MidWeek* magazine. Also in the works: a series of seminars about "making a difference." It's my hope that these commentaries (and seminars) will strike a nerve, helping people realize that we can, and should, strive to make a positive impact somehow, some way.

I thank my parents, Alice and Arthur, for instilling this concept in me at a tender age. Stand up for what's right, fight for the underdog, question authority, live with empathy and passion (not drama), serve in whatever capacity you can. I had wonderful role models for parents in so many ways, and I am also blessed to have two great sisters, Sue and Margaret, an incredible and supportive wife, Shari, three great kids—Michael, Megan, and David—a tremendous daughter-in-law, Desi, and two (so far) ever-evolving grandkids, Alex and Benji. Not to mention a full roster of extended family and friends in so many arenas and places—work, public service, media, sports, college, high school, and grammar school. Business mentors have included Dennis Minga, Jeff Coelho, John Hayes, Paul McTear, Rick Blangiardi, and Wayne Daugherty. Hell, I've even had a great run with the family dogs throughout my life: Archie, Brandy, Morgan, Buffy, Casey, Sadie, and Ryelee!

I do hope you find something in these pages that resonates with you, that causes your inner soul to stir, that allows you to not only "think about it," but to go out and do it!

Aloha,

John 2. Fink

March 2, 2000

Introducing "Think About It…"

Every week right here, I will be giving you 60 seconds of information. Opinions, stories, anecdotes, or editorials. The topics will vary from week to week, message to message. The name of this one-minute feature will be "Think About It…"

The purpose of "Think About It…" will be to give the people of Hawai'i food for thought. I don't pretend to have all the answers. But I can certainly ask the questions and, sometimes, give a point of view—in order for people to just "think about it."

As general manager of News 8 (KHNL) and K5 The Home Team (KFVE), I take my responsibility as a corporate citizen very seriously, and I do feel it is important to communicate. We live in a world that moves awfully fast. Hopefully, these one-minute moments will allow people to reflect on what's going on, and at the end of the day, maybe we can make changes or acknowledge actions that are making a difference in Hawai'i.

As for feedback, I encourage you to e-mail me, write to me, or visit our website. Again, the goal is for people to talk, to communicate, to understand, to think about it…

And *"think about it"* we did, for 19 years and almost 2,000 editorials!

March 24, 2000

Technology

With all of the great strides mankind keeps making in the world of technology, it is vital to keep this uncharted world of fast-paced, technological tools in perspective.

Nowadays, you can be beeped, buzzed, paged, called, voice-mailed, emailed, and faxed 24 hours a day seven days a week. Some kids spend more time in chat rooms and on websites than they do talking to each other face-to-face. Not to mention actually speaking with their own parents. Many kids think that correct spelling is an inalienable right given to them through "spell-check" on a computer.

This is not good! Nothing beats human interaction. We all need downtime, quiet time where you shouldn't have to worry about being accessible or in constant touch. Don't let the tools of technology make you a slave to the machines. Technology is a pathway to help us, but it cannot be the driver. Think about it…

Twenty years later, some people consider their cell phones to be appendages; some live and die for "likes" and "followers." More than 90% of adults have a cell phone within arm's length at all times. Ugh.

February 7, 2001

Gambling

A year ago, a proposal came forward for shipboard gambling. It never left the legislative dock. Now there has been talk of setting up a lone casino site as an experiment. It makes for a good story, but it's got as much chance of winning lawmakers' approval as the San Diego Chargers have to win the 2002 Super Bowl.

Let's face it. Hawai'i has gambling—Hawai'i people spend millions in Las Vegas. And that's their choice. Plus, the Vegas lobby does a nice job of making sure folks from Hawai'i keep going there by using great packages and local specials. Of course, we do have illegal betting in Hawai'i, which many people simply wink at and accept to some degree. Some people eat too much, some drink too much, and some drive poorly but we don't ban those activities because of possible abuse.

To not allow even one highly controlled, highly regulated casino experiment on the Big Island, Moloka'i, or on a cruise ship seems to be another way to simply ensure status quo in Hawai'i: underfunded education, underground gambling, and lots of local people winging off to Las Vegas. Think about it…

Now that the Supreme Court has lifted the federal ban on sports gambling, leaving it up to each state to decide, 11 states (as of fall 2019) have legalized local sports betting, more than 20 states have legislation pending, and about 10 additional states are considering sports betting legislation. What are the odds we'll see something here?

September 14, 2001

Why?

Why? The question continues to be asked by our children and our friends. Why do bad things happen to good people? How could something like this happen? We are vulnerable, this we now know for sure. We must become better prepared, better educated, and more alert. In the land of the free, we can never take that freedom for granted again. What a horrible wake-up call. What a ghastly way to realize that everything isn't going to be the way it was before Tuesday. And something will be done. Someone must pay.

Many people have suggested that the repeated images of the World Trade Center explosions are almost surreal and numbing images, like something we've seen in the movies. But it's not a movie. It's real. Perhaps we can take small consolation in realizing that, like in many movies, good will prevail over evil, right will win out over wrong, and justice will be served. That you can count on these days when many of our values and sensibilities have been shaken, but not broken. We will not be broken. Think about it…

The incidents of 9/11/01 will live in Infamy forever. It changed our world in many ways, and perhaps made all of us feel a bit naïve in retrospect. It was truly one of the hardest weeks in my professional life, and even with 72 straight hours of network and local news coverage, it still seemed to be a bad dream that wouldn't go away.

Think about it..

January 11, 2002

Parking Perils

There is a nefarious parking conundrum seen throughout Hawai'i. You notice it in mall parking lots when you see car paint on all of the tight walls.

You notice it when you can't open the door of your car because the ignorant car-parker next to you went over the dividing line in his or her rush.

You notice it when you see half the parking lot signs assigned to compact cars, and yet everything from trucks to minivans are loaded into those precious spaces. Even spaces not marked "compact" are best reserved for mopeds or motorcycles.

The lines seem to be closing in on us, and with the prevalence and sales records of sport utility vehicles, minivans, and trucks on Hawai'i's roads, the answer may be to either lose weight so you can squeeze out of your car or plan to park further away, where the deer and the antelope play (and no one else will ding your car).

Space is at a costly premium in Hawai'i, even in parking lots, and it seems as if the lines are moving in on us. Maybe it's time to walk, ride a bike, or take the bus. Think about it…

Trucks, SUVs, CUVs, and minivans combined now outsell cars here annually by about 58% to 42%, and those parking spaces seem to get smaller and smaller…

Think about it.

May 15, 2002

Kaiser Kudos

There was a great Spike Lee movie called "Do the Right Thing" a number of years ago. Too often, we as a society tend to focus on things not being done right: people doing wrong, institutions being unfair, the world in a horrific spiral. "What is up with humanity?" we may ask in 2002 as we look around the troubled globe.

Well, three students at Kaiser High School did the right thing. They showed integrity. They called themselves on an error that adult math contest judges overlooked, and thus deprived themselves of winning the state math contest, after the three had been notified that they had finished in first place. Certainly it was the right thing to do. But that's not obvious to some people.

It's OK to celebrate when people do right, when people show virtues and principles—especially teenagers—in an era of stereotyping slackers and dropouts and pointing out youthful transgressions and imperfections. In this case, three teenagers decided that integrity and honesty were more important than winning a first place trophy. And that is truly the essence of winning. Think about it…

Think about it.

February 5, 2003

Aloha (to the) Stadium

By current marketplace standards, Aloha Stadium is an obsolete facility. It is not the fault of the planners or the current management. It's simply the result of being 27 years old and in need of too much repair. The parking situation cannot be fixed as things currently stand. There is no more room. There are no corporate luxury boxes, a surefire moneymaker.

And pouring more bad money after good money for years of repair is shortsighted and does not solve the numerous problems that cause potential fans to stay away in droves. Tearing the stadium down and putting up a new one in Hālawa will take years for planning, destruction, and construction. And what would UH do during the year of repair work? Play its home games on the road or on Maui? Or do we build a new stadium now in Kapolei or in Mānoa?

Decisions need to be made quickly, but the thought of a fan-friendly stadium with corporate-funded luxury boxes, ample parking, easy access, and quality food sure sounds like the right plan for the 21st century. Think about it…

Good news! The plan is in place, and hopefully UH will be playing in its new home in 2023 or 2024, with all of the amenities and comforts you would hope for in a modern facility. And on site there should be a parking structure, a retail area, housing, and perhaps even a hotel to help pay for it all going forward.

May 28, 2003

Graduated Advice

As we enter the happy season of graduation, everyone is going to be full of advice. Obvious but necessary advice is to remind you to celebrate in moderation—please, don't become a news story by making a youthful indiscretion at some party. Advice-givers will tell you to make the most of your opportunities, to live life to its fullest, to give back to your community.

You will be advised to reach your potential, to set goals, to strive to be all that you can be. Now all of these are sound and sagely words of wisdom, and you will undoubtedly hear more words to the wise from your classmates, family, and school administrators. Well, here are my two cents.

Laugh. Have fun. Make room for some joy in your life every day. Have a good sense of humor and a better sense of perspective about everything. Be serious about your work, but not about yourself. Humor is vital for your physical well-being, your psyche, and your demeanor. So make sure you laugh a lot as you move on. Life is a whoopee cushion; sit on it. Think about it…

July 7, 2004

Working Hard, Or Hardly Working

Hawai'i now has the lowest unemployment rate of any state in the country. That's great news, but it probably won't last forever. So keep this in mind. What employers look for in good times and in bad are quality workers, passionate workers, caring workers, multitalented workers. Employers don't simply need or want people who just show up every day, punch in and punch out, but really do nothing to enhance an organization's performance.

Are you an asset to your company or workplace? Are you perceived to be a valuable employee who works well with people, brings new ideas to the table, and helps the company meet or exceed its goals?

Or do you think the company owes you; that simply being there every day is good enough? Actually, if you're not happy or fulfilled at work, now might be a good time to look elsewhere, since demand exceeds supply. But do yourself and everyone around you a favor—be good or be gone. No one individual owes you a living. We don't need more workers in Hawai'i, we need more dedicated, quality, passionate workers. Think about it…

Well, nowadays we do need more specific expertise in certain fields—nurses, teachers, digital specialists—but we still need passionate (not dramatic) and committed workers, as always. Find and feed your passion.

Graffiti

Why must people spread their supposed artwork all over public places and deface property? I refuse to call these people "artists," because commercial artists usually exist for some higher purpose like a salary or at least some cultural pleasure.

But why do people feel the need to tag parking structures, new walls, school buildings, street signs, etc.? Why don't these people do something productive with their artwork capabilities, like volunteer time to tutor young kids or maybe even design a new UH campus logo?

Obviously, these spray paint design wizards have sleeping issues, too, since most, if not all, of their work is done in the dead of the night. Well, I'll tell you what, Michelangelo, the costs and residual effects of you ruining our signs, personal property, and buildings are not worth your thrill-seeking sense and self-fulfillment sense. So put the spray can back in your pocket, and go do something productive with your free time and ideas. Think about it...

May 13, 2005

Home Run

How do you buy a home in Hawai'i nowadays? Seems like every week the median price keeps going north, while salaries and new job opportunities certainly don't move that quickly. The only refreshing note is that we always hear about the median price for homes on O'ahu or Maui. "Median" means that while half the home prices are higher, half are also lower, so there is still some hope for people just getting going on home-owning, or those looking for upgrades from their current residence.

If all of the homes and condos being built are upscale and in the million dollar plus range, the median price will continue to rise, but the lower priced houses will still be there. Unfortunately, someone will already be living in those homes, and that's why we need to see more so-called "affordable" homes being built. If not, we will continue to see young professionals abandon Hawai'i due to the limitations in housing and higher-paying jobs elsewhere. "What goes up must come down" is the old adage. But at these home prices, will anyone be left for a bottom end that's still too high for most middle-income consumers? Think about it...

Looks like we're still in the same place 15 years later—and now we're losing population.

November 16, 2005

Affordable Grousing

What is "affordable housing" and who's responsible for making sure we have enough of it to allow the younger generations to live here in the future? Will we drive people away who realize that they can never own their own home in Hawai'i, or will some entrepreneur figure out a way to make a fair profit and yet still provide truly affordable homes to the disconnected people who simply cannot buy these days? Is Hawai'i becoming even more of a land of haves and have-nots, a civilization of people who have family money or top jobs who have housing, and an up-and-coming group that simply cannot even play the real estate game?

If the American dream includes buying a home, can there possibly be a realistic solution out there for the so-called middle class in Hawai'i who simply cannot play when median prices are at $590,000? If more homes are being built further away from the work center in Honolulu, will the pipe dream mass transit be built in enough time to allow these people a realistic route to work that doesn't take two hours a day?

Hopefully all of this will come together and work out, or the disenchanted ones will be gone, and the aging population of Hawai'i will have even larger social problems 20 years from now. Think about it...

The median price for a single-family home on O'ahu is now over $800,000. And it's actually been over 14 years since this was written and aired, not 20, but the social problems are in plain sight as the younger generation is in "plane" sight—leaving for the mainland!

January 6, 2006

Tourism Boom or Boon?

       2005 set a record for the number of tourists that visited our islands. While arrivals from Japan were down two percent, arrivals from the continent were up over eight percent, including Canadian guests. Regardless of your view on whether this is more of a good thing or whether we are reaching the saturation point from an infrastructure standpoint, one thing is for sure: we still need to find supplemental economic boosters to drive our economy beyond basic tourism and military spending.

       Entrepreneurs and others must find a few more cogs to keep our economic engine purring. Sports tourism, ecotourism, and other offshoots of the basic visitor stereotype are having a nice effect to grow tourism into its current King Kong–like seven million strong edition in 2005. And that's great. But we really must continue to look at island nations and other places that have evolved beyond a one-trick economy. We all know what the downside is if and when things slow down. Let's make sure everything is being done to keep the economy moving ahead. After all, it affects everybody here at some level. Think about it...

Tourism records continue to get broken, and some suggest our infrastructure is following.

Race Relations

After 42 years, Hawaii Raceway Park will close in a few months. Whether or not you care about a legitimate racing site for those who feel the need for speed is beside the point. The fact that there is a sanctioned venue for car and motor sport enthusiasts is the bottom line, and something needs to be set up quickly to keep the cars and racers in a safe zone, so to speak.

People are going to race their vehicles. At least with a legal site like Hawaii Raceway Park, the adrenaline rush of racing has been confined to an area established for this purpose. As it looks like the raceway park simply cannot overcome the cesspool problems that are causing this closure, racers and fans are without a location to rev it up. There is talk about still saving this site. Other development ideas have simply not come to fruition, and the clock is really ticking now.

We can talk all we want about educating drivers about racing in our streets, but without a place to ramp up the RPMs, the fear is that highway and side street incidents will increase, and that's not a promising thought for anyone. Here's hoping for an amenable solution real soon. Think about it…

Fourteen years later, and we still await a solution that might just give testosterone-d highway daredevils a safer place to ply their weaving skills.

21

March 10, 2006

Streets of Woe

I don't know if the formula for our roads is something out of the chocolate factory in Willy Wonka, but since it rains here a bit every year, and since our roads seem to crumble at an alarming rate, even after being freshly paved, is it possible that the ingredients need to be revisited? Must the Pali and Nimitz and Kapiʻolani always be in a state of disrepair?

Is it possible that more expensive roadway material could save more money over the long haul, as repairs would be needed less often? What do Seattle or Portland use to keep the roads there in decent shape? Boston gets a lot of moisture annually—is there a better way? A lot of the US gets more than its fair share of rain, sleet, and snow every year; do they have constant and repeated road woes?

Maybe the stuff we're using really is the best option, but try telling that to your mechanic when the car alignment gets thrown out of whack, again. Of course, the bumps and ruts help to keep him in business. Think about it...

Word is that asphalt recently installed on the Pali Highway is an upgrade from the previous silly putty, and it was successfully used on the Moanalua Freeway way back in 2004! We'll see.

North Sure

Some people want the country to stay country. Other people want a job with growth opportunities close to home. Some see expansion on the North Shore as a huge plus, a chance to make a close-knit community into a thriving, entrepreneurial entity. Others see it as the beginning of the end—a permanent change, if it comes about, to the last bastion of rural O'ahu and the Hawai'i of old.

The pending development plans around Turtle Bay and Kawela Bay promise to bring the emotion and logic of many groups to the front—local residents, ecologists, marine biologists, traffic specialists, developers, etc. Hopefully, the community can work with the developers to decide what is in the best interests of the people who will be most affected, future inhabitants who might call this changed area home.

Of course, residents may choose not to stay if they don't like the outcome of this plan and what it means with the planned development or without the development. Any approaches must be carefully coordinated with progressive thinking about those who will be most affected by this upcoming massive project: the generations to come. Think about it...

Still waiting...

Think about it.

March 24, 2006

Plane Truth

Within the next year, you might actually be able to use a cell phone on an airplane. Frankly, that's horrible news. The last thing we need is for some yapper next to us to be babbling during the five-hour flight from Hawai'i to the West Coast. As technology and safety concerns are addressed, the mere fact that we can talk via cell phone during flights should not overcome the obvious concerns about private space and your right to peace and quiet.

Right now, when your over-anxious new plane buddy starts talking about the latest Woody Allen flick, you can simply close your eyes and he or she will get the hint. But just imagine if everyone can now spend a majority of the flight overanalyzing the never-ending plight of the llama as a beast of burden with their friend in Peru for four hours! "Uh...excuse me, flight attendant, but can I get off of this flight in midair?"

Just because we can do something through the wonders of technology does not always mean we must, or should. Please, keep your cell phone in your pocket at least until we reach the gate if this modern-day wonder comes true, unless the White House needs you. Think about it...

Think about it

Grandparents Day and 9/11

Sunday is Grandparents Day throughout the country, Tūtū Day in Hawai'i, and it would be an appropriate time to remind your parents how much you appreciate what they do and mean to your kids. Perhaps a sincere handwritten card from the kiddies would be a nice touch, too. After all, if it wasn't for our grandparents, where would we be? Right, we wouldn't exist.

Monday marks five years since that tragic day of terror—September 11, 2001. It will be a day filled with solemn recollecting and melancholy pondering about how our lives and thinking in general have changed since that infamous day. It might be an especially appropriate time to remember your loved ones, telling them how much you really do care, from great aunts to spouses to grandparents.

The world and the issues that influence our lives might very well be more confusing than ever, but we can still smile with and hold and love those around us who help us stay sane and centered...not the worst thought heading into Grandparents Day and the fifth anniversary of 9/11. Think about it...

September 6, 2006

Sweet Home Alabama

I had the pleasure of spending five days in Alabama this past week, and if you think we have the patent or monopoly on "aloha spirit," let me assure you, it's alive and well in the form of down-home Southern hospitality in Alabama.

Like when we were asked to tailgate with people we had never met before, people who fed us and laughed with us before and after the game. Like when the local sheriff stopped directing traffic and got into his car to help lead us to our tailgating destination on the congested Tuscaloosa campus. Like when four or five different Alabama fans saw my University of Hawai'i logo-ed shirt and went out of their way to thank me for coming to their state as they also hoped I was enjoying my stay—and this was before the football game when the outcome was obviously still in doubt! Almost 100,000 people, no alcohol in the stadium, and a wonderful, collegiate atmosphere for sure.

I wonder if we treat our bright-eyed visitors this well when we see them here. I wonder if we talk about friendliness and caring more than we sometimes show it. Something to ponder, but I do know that there really is deep meaning and reality to that storied Lynyrd Skynyrd phrase, "Sweet home Alabama." Think about it...

October 20, 2006

Why-pio?

Something has happened to the lush soccer park known as the Waipiʻo Soccer Peninsula. It is falling into disrepair. The finest park for playing ball in Hawaiʻi has been pruned immaculately for years, but is now starting to look like all of the others. And that's not good. Clumps of weeds, brown spots due to overuse or lack of timely watering, bathroom stalls out of order for weeks on end.

Why must this pristine, well-thought-of area fall into the spiral of so many other local parks? Waipio is not overused every day like too many other parks throughout Oʻahu, so why can't we keep this one from going down the road to ruin?

Waipiʻo has been a recreational and economic bright spot over the years with national soccer tournaments for kids and adults, and will certainly be used again, unless these fields become dust piles and splotchy, bumpy pitches like those in play at Kapiʻolani Park, Ala Wai, Waiʻalae Iki, Kapāolono, Crane, Waiau, Mōʻiliʻili, and numerous other sites. This park was intended to be used wisely, carefully, and should be showcased for years. Don't let it become yet another sorry, eroded patch. Please, think about it...

UH Wahine games postponed or moved in recent years say it all—the main playing arena and its adjacent fields have joined many others on Oʻahu in relative disrepair, neglect, and/or overuse.

Think about it.

November 10, 2006

Veterans Values

Tomorrow is Veterans Day, a day to honor all of America's war veterans. It is a day meant to humbly honor and acknowledge those who have fought for our liberties. Whether or not you believe in the policies and political posturing that puts our nation's military in harm's way from time to time, these are people we are acknowledging tomorrow, not policies, parties, or posturing. November 11 is a poignant moment in time for everyone to realize that there is a price for freedom and for the many things we have that we take for granted in our country.

Veterans Day is not about political sides. It's not about mindless media pundits who make their living through overhyped exaggerations and generalizations by gnawing on and driving a wedge in the differences in belief systems throughout this country, a country that has always tolerated different beliefs and viewpoints. Keep in mind, we were founded by unhappy dissidents.

There really are no red states or blue states. There are shades in between everywhere. Perhaps all states are really purple with a bunch of kinda red people and a bunch of kinda blue people. But veterans do the job they are required to do; in the end, they have no color, they work for all of us. Thank them tomorrow, and think about it...

Copper Caper

An emailer last week suggested that I act like I'm "holier than thou" in my commentaries. Far from it; I like to think I'm just one of the guys talking about what's going on. But some people are never satisfied. Well, this week I'm pleased to talk about a nifty neighborhood nabbing.

Yes, I'm now going to steal (pardon the pun) from an old Johnny Carson/Jack Webb "Tonight Show" routine. It was great to see that police grabbed malevolent metal thieves last week. That's right, concerned cops caught a couple of creeps calculating a copper caper. The copper culprits got collared because they didn't comply with the current code. The "cash for copper" collaborators couldn't figure out that the heavy HECO spool was hot. Hard to handle, yeah?

Now the key for cops and consumers is a quick conviction and concrete consequences for these cocky copper keepers. We can't continue to coddle crooks, as we must convince cocky conspirators to keep their cotton-pickin' hands off of our copper construction, which will keep consumers content and stop these copper-copping cases. Think about it...

Think about it.

Hot Box

The state of Hawaiʻi is spending $23,000 to make sure that the hottest public schools get first dibs on air-conditioning. Boy, I would hate to be there when one school gets put on the waiting list because it's only 84.3 degrees inside, instead of the 84.5 degrees it takes to make the magic list. I sure hope the thermometers are accurate and the tests are all done around 1 p.m.

Let's be real, we need immediate answers to sauna-like classrooms if we expect to teach the kids anything beyond weight loss on a regular basis. No child left behind? How about no child melting? Seriously, how about some public–private entrepreneurial ideas like solar ceiling fans or a donation of fans, or how about some creative fundraisers, sad as it may be, like they did at Kalaheo High School. And I think it was just a year or so ago that a Kalaheo teacher held a fundraiser to get enough books for the students in her class.

Public school is really a year-round issue throughout most of Hawaiʻi, so this heat issue is not about to let up. Find the funds for fans, if the wildly expensive air-conditioning plans simply can't be done. Unlike mass transit and a few other forever projects, this sad situation cannot be put on the back burner; it's on the front burner every day in ʻEwa, Campbell, Kīhei, Kailua, etc. Think about it…

Well, it took another decade to get action taken, but more kids are now getting air as we've gotten beyond the redundant political hot air pontificating about "our keiki are our future" while we let them roast in classrooms…for over 30 years.

May 14, 2007

Mother May I?

I hope you're as lucky as I am. I hope Mother's Day had some deeper meaning to you than just a card or a phone call. I hope you had someone to really thank, or someone to really remember with a great sense of fondness and love, with some specific memories of happiness. And if you had difficulties with dear old mom and she's gone, it's not too late to simply say, "I know you did your best, Mom." Yeah, moms are humans, too.

I hope that you were brought into this world by someone who makes it easy for you to say thank you to not just once a year. I hope you take time in the coming weeks and months to spend a little extra time with your aging mom. I hope the words "I love ya, Mom" come easily to you. Please, you don't have to wait for the annual commercial reminder from Hallmark cards next May. Mark your calendar to do something nice next week or next month.

I hope that the words you said last week and wrote down for Mom to read were sincere and meaningful. There is no greater love than that of a parent, and it is silly to compartmentalize your affection for one day, once a year. If every day is children's day, as we used to hear as kids, then there's no reason that all of us can't find the time to make sure that Mother's Day comes around a bit more often through our actions and our words. Think about it...

Sadly, my mom passed away as I was working on this book. She was an incredible and giving woman who felt that reading was an integral part of helping to ensure that our keiki have a better chance to succeed later in life. As usual, she was right!

May 16, 2007

Ho Hmm

I interviewed Don Ho almost 30 years ago for a local magazine. It was before his show, and he let me into his dressing room and made me feel right at home. Twenty-five years later, an entertainment friend of mine was in town and wanted to go to Don's show, so we went, and we met up with Don right before the show. Again, he couldn't have been more pleasant, more personable, more real.

The entertainment industry locally and nationally is full of prima donnas, wannabes, egos out of control, what's-in-it-for-mes, but something was very noble about the way Don went about his craft, the way he humbly accepted whatever fame came his way. Maybe it's the ultimate example of local style, his "ain't no big thing" mantra. Maybe it was his deep understanding of his true roots. Maybe it was the fact that he simply connected with the audience while never taking himself too seriously. Maybe we can all learn from that—connect, but relax.

Don Ho was the last great act of a bygone era, and he truly made a difference to millions of visitors and TV viewers who considered him a local icon as big as Diamond Head. He shared his gift, and like all gifts, some loved it, some didn't. Either way, it surely "ain't no big thing." Think about it.

Singer Don Ho passed away on April 14, 2007, prompting this editorial.

Think about it.

Hawai'i 20/20

A Hawai'i 2050 sustainability summit in Waikīkī was held recently. A lot of great ideas emanating from more than a year's worth of meetings were put into a draft plan that the state legislature will hopefully massage as it looks into future legislation. This is all well and good, but a plan that will be a defined roadmap over the next 43 years sure seems like a lifetime of emptiness. What about a Hawai'i 2020 plan? You know, like 20/20 vision, something that would be clear with measurable goals every year for the next decade or so. Something that we could all watch evolve carefully, not something that won't be realized for two generations.

General concepts and items to address are relatively easy to identify. The difficulty is in the details, the ramifications, the effects. Housing issues, community character, natural resource utilization, and quality of life issues in Hawai'i are ongoing topics this week, next month, and will continue to be in 43 years. Frankly, some of us don't have that long to wait for some answers, nor do our kids, or their kids.

Hawai'i 2020 would certainly force certain actionable items at the governmental and community levels now. Hawai'i 2020 would allow a realistic timeline, yet allow for benchmarks and checkpoints along the way every year or two, not every decade or two. The time is now to continue the research, the committee ideas, the community concerns and comments, and let's make sustainability and quality of life decisions an ongoing project that has quantifiable goals, champions, and deadlines. Or, for the next couple of decades, we can just think about it.

It's now 2020. How's the plan looking for this year, let alone for 2050?

Think about it...

December 24, 2007

Ho Ho Hum

Why can't it last? I mean the spirit, the decorations, the jovial camaraderie, the good tidings and all. Why must we let a short season and a calendar dictate our actions and reactions? Is it really that hard for the human species to be upbeat, vibrant, forgiving, pleasant, and understanding for more than about two straight weeks a year? Is it that tough to tidy things up and put eye candy around to make our sometimes mundane surroundings look a bit spiffier now and again? We tend to be a civil sort in Hawai'i, but can we do better more often? Of course we can.

I understand and embrace the deeper implications of Christmas, but we sure do it up with displays and gifts and everything else, which really don't dig below the surface of "feel good." OK, so without the gifts and the excess of food, how about if we all make it our resolution to carry this spirit, this concept, this sensibility into more of a year-round affair? Good tidings, peace on earth, joy to the world—we don't really need just an abbreviated season for that now do we?

Can we try to evolve to a point where this stuff really has longevity and meaning beyond the dates we've been given? I don't know, maybe it is too much to ask everyone to relax a bit, enjoy their fellow man, etc., etc., all the time. But isn't that part of what this season is about: hopeful wish lists? Merry Christmas. Think about it.

Think about it.

January 16, 2008

System Failure

There's an old saying: "If it ain't broke don't fix it." But in Hawai'i, we have a hard time agreeing on what exactly is broke. And then, sometimes, we just talk about it, ignore it, and don't fix it. It doesn't take an engineer or an architect or even a state legislator to know that the physical plants in which our students and student athletes are supposed to learn and train are woefully run down. Dashed hopes, false promises, delayed responses, it all comes to the same ending often times—nothing gets done and certainly nothing gets done quickly.

We have a habit here of building things and people up, and then if everything doesn't work out we blame the institution or the individual. Well how about looking at the system; the system that allows mediocrity to fester. We talk about the importance of education, and then we stand by idly while passionate teachers run their own fundraisers or spend their own money to buy supplies in order to get by. We want a topflight, competitive athletic department at UH, but we refuse to simply meet the industry standards for infrastructure and recruiting and assistant coach pay. So big-picture questions: Do we dare raise taxes so kids have pipes that work in every school and air that's not 100 degrees? Do we save money by cutting back local government, perhaps looking at a unicameral system vs. having a House and a Senate? Do we have the nerve to stop feeling sorry for ourselves or inferior to the mainland in so many ways? Do we dare cut bureaucracy or force things to move quicker?

We have great people all over the place at the University of Hawai'i, but this month we're stunned because we've lost a great football coach. He gave the system ten years. You wanna question his loyalty, the fact that he simply couldn't tolerate annual expectations to win just about every game with a perceived lack of support? He had options, and maybe you don't; maybe you're OK just accepting status quo or worse. He wasn't willing to; he had more local sensibility and soul than a lot of people we all know who were born and raised here. And now, he's gone. And that's a tough wake-up call. Maybe we'll wake up and move forward, because right now it's a bad dream. And I don't just mean this football thing. Think about it.

The UH football coach referenced here was June Jones.

January 1, 2008

Big Easy Aloha

It seems like a lifetime ago, but three weeks ago, more than 15,000 local UH football fans roamed the streets and restaurants and hotels of New Orleans. It was a godsend for a city still deeply struggling with that force of Mother Nature and human error known as Hurricane Katrina. It also came at a time when New Orleans kept its top slot as the murder capital of America, per capita. The gracious guests from Hawai'i, with the big-time need for omiyage and such, certainly provided a brief respite as the Big Easy tries valiantly not to be perceived as the "big queasy."

It was amazing to see so many friendly, but chilly, local faces around town. Ti leaves and green beads became standard gear for the visitors and their mainland friends and relatives. In retrospect, no way could this tightly knit group have stayed so close as a single, cohesive, passionate, excited unit had UH been sent to the Rose Bowl or the Fiesta Bowl. For three or four days, New Orleans became our easternmost island, and it was a wonderful way to end the year. Southern hospitality combined with aloha spirit created a jambalaya of spicy and meaty memories for attendees in that short, sweet week.

Of course, we know what happened in the News Year's Day football game…but it might have been more than just a game, it might have actually been a much-needed wake-up call. Hawai'i fans answered the call down in New Orleans and left behind a lot of good feelings and money. Hopefully, we all brought something more back home. Think about it.

Think about it.

February 4, 2008

Inter-Networks

The other day I heard someone talking about some fact they had found and when queried on their proof about the subject, they nonchalantly replied that they had read it on the internet. Now I think the internet is really cool and fun and useful and informative for myriad reasons, but just because you see something on the internet, be careful about assuming its veracity. Anyone can put stuff on the web—matter of fact, millions of people do. That's part of the appeal and part of the danger. When it comes to getting information and facts, we must all be independent auditors to check the sources.

From political exposés to rumors to edited pictures to sick predators lurking behind veiled disguises online, the internet is truly the people's communication tool—of the people, by the people, and for the people. But that doesn't make it right all the time, and that doesn't ensure that the information we get is factual and fair. One of the things mainstream media are supposed to do for all of us is to check the facts, check the sources, get corroborating information before going public. It is a journalist's job to go through the vetting process to ensure the imparting of correct information. "Better to be right than simply to be first with the story" is a mantra that one hopes responsible journalists abide by. If we don't do our jobs, then change the channel or don't buy the newspaper.

So stay informed and have fun with the wonderful worldwide web, but be careful with what you learn unless you are comfortable with where and from whom it came. And keep an eye on the kids, please. Think about it.

And here we are, 12 years later. Misuse of and misinformation on the internet is worse than ever. Trolls rule and monolithic digital companies reap billions of dollars on their backs. Digital devotees crave "friends", "likes", "and "thumbs up" for acceptance; cyberbullies run amok; and false information spreads like wildfire. Well, it sure seemed like a good idea at first.

March 10, 2008

Somebody Get Me a Doctor

We're purportedly running out of doctors in Hawai'i. Well, at least in some areas, there is a dangerous shortage of specialists and even general practitioners, which also invariably means that the docs handling the load are working too long and probably too hard. Mistakes do happen, and doctors are human, too. Reasons given for the physician shortage include the cost of insurance for practitioners, the cutbacks in reimbursements from insurance companies, and the general cost of doing business in Hawai'i.

Scoff at this problem at your own risk, literally, because one day you might make a call and find out that nobody's home, or in the office. It's the rural areas, the windward side, the Neighbor Islands; the spread of this doctor shortage is being felt all over our state. Would you believe that Maui is the only Neighbor Island with even one neurosurgeon?! I guess you wouldn't know that until you really needed it, which might be too late. Perhaps this cry of concern in Hawai'i is simply our local anguish as part of the nationwide plague that is known as the decaying health-care system. Like a tough-to-stop necrosis, it's eating away at our society, and with an aging population it's not going away. It's a big election year issue, and maybe Hawai'i's legislators and professional organizations—medical and insurance—can lead the way to finding some methodology to at least slow down the increasing number of "Closed" signs at doctor's offices in Hawai'i. Think about it…

March 24, 2008

Ex-cede-ingly Slow

Some things take forever to change or get fixed in Hawai'i. Actually, a lot of things simply take too long. But the ridiculous state, or lack thereof, of a decision on ceded revenue for the Native Hawaiian Trust has now been awaiting a ruling for three decades. That's 30 years, folks, and the powers that be and the influencers and the recipients have all had undue amounts of time and meetings and pleas to get this thing settled.

Bottom line—well, that's the whole point—the bottom line. How much should be paid, and when and how? But after 30 years, isn't a rational decision that obviously involves some consensus and some compromise due? If people and impassioned recipients are going to give testimony and opinion and try to resolve this, isn't that the purpose of the legislature—to make decisions?

In an election year, the "wrong" decision, whatever that might be, will certainly be unpopular, under the heading that you can't please all of the people all of the time, and a legislator's number one job is to retain his or her job. But 30 years and no end result or start of payments in sight? And it's not like this issue just popped up this session. Let's hope the state House can bring this bill back to the front. Let's find out who is keeping it from happening and try to get some resolution—again, somebody isn't going to be happy no matter what. That's how things tend to work in a democracy. It's never unanimous. Think about it...

April 7, 2008

Aloha Means Goodbye

Aloha means goodbye. Goodbye to 61 years of service; goodbye to over 1,900 employees; goodbye to a reliable and viable option for local travelers; goodbye to an airline, which began, in part, to offer equal opportunities to minorities.

While the airline wars have been fierce and unfriendly of late, did you ever think that Aloha Airlines would join the list of defunct Hawai'i air carriers, alongside MidPacific, Discovery, and Mahalo Airlines? The jet fuel prices, the cost of doing business, the questioned practices of a third player—it all added up to bankruptcy for the second time in the past four years, and this time it results in a complete shutdown of passenger service.

Last ditch efforts to find a financier or buyer failed, and certainly the nationwide credit crunch made the timing of this announcement even worse in terms of finding an eleventh-hour savior. The accusations of unfair competition will continue, as will the Aloha lawsuit against Go! Airlines, and 1,900 residents will hopefully find something real soon to allow them to move ahead with their lives, which they must. Aloha meant "hello" in our skies almost 62 years ago; aloha meant "love" to the many employees and passengers; and now, sadly, aloha truly does mean "goodbye." Think about it...

Think about it

April 23, 2008

Gem-uflecting

Another jewel in the pantheon of small businesses calling it quits was announced last week. Kakesako Brothers Jewelers has been a downtown landmark for 58 years, and now it will be closing. The passing of Tommy Kakesako last August and the difficulty in keeping the family-owned business going means that we are losing a true gem. The people at Kakesako— Tommy, Robin, Margie, and all of the friendly staff—made shopping for jewelry a charm.

Take it from someone who's not a huge fan of shopping nor a real expert on fashion and style, a trip to Kakesako made everyone feel cared for, listened to, and valued. Tommy was a member of the vaunted 442nd Regiment, I Company, and he was a dear friend to my family for the past 30 years. He had the true spirit of caring, defined 'ohana, and possessed a depth of soul that always shone through his quiet, passive demeanor.

I will always cherish my memories of Tommy sitting there with his magnifying monocle, fixing a watch or tweaking a bracelet's insides. He was a peaceful warrior, a credit to his country and his industry, and a pal to my late dad. We need more Kakesakos out there, in many places, in all of our lives, and this retail jewelry establishment is a local diamond in the rough that will surely be missed. Think about it...

July 21, 2008

Whale Tale

It took a while, but a whale was wheeled away last week after weighing in for weeks and having its stench wafting for quite a while. Whale, whale. After weeks of wallowing on the shore, wary workers wenched the washed-up whale while watchers winced, and some almost wilted. Pilau! The wind worked to widen the width of the whale's stench, thus adding to the woes of the watchers in the neighborhood.

When this wondrous creature wasted away while watchers wheezed and waves worried the workers, one wonders why this woeful whale tale occurred in the first place. Hopefully, the wise wizards of whale-ology can learn from this magnificent 65-foot-long denizen of the deep; these beautiful and gigantic creatures, almost mythical in nature, are sometimes taken for granted as their numbers decline worldwide.

While you may not wail for this whale, woe unto us all if we become callous and oblivious to the plight of majestic animals such as this one or even less revered creatures of the planet. Perhaps the fate of other species, due to our arrogance, ignorance, or indifference, will invariably make our plight on this planet a precarious one in the centuries ahead. Think about it...

Think about it.

August 13, 2008

Higher, Faster, Stronger

Recently I saw the tale of an aspiring golf professional who had dreams and aspirations of greatness. Then, his golf cart overturned, severely damaging his spinal cord and leaving him paralyzed from the waist down. Now, for the past 33 years, he has given instructional golf seminars and hit balls from crazy angles with weird-looking clubs. He has his capable dog, Benji Hogan, tee up balls for him and has amazed kids and adults for years with his actions and his anecdotes. He has overcome fear, pain, anger, depression, prejudice, and resentment. This is a tale of truly Olympic proportions.

Basically, Dennis Walters reinvented himself. Now 58 years old, Dennis, with amazing help and love from his father, has taken his 1974 life-altering tragedy and turned it upside down. The show that Walters puts on is not really about golf. It's about life. It's about rebounding from a big curveball. It's about persevering, attempting, and ultimately attaining a new goal. He can hit a golf ball over 200 yards, sometimes blindfolded. His friend, former New York Yankees pitcher, Ralph Terry, who was with him that fateful day, said a few years back, "I think life isn't about what you achieve, it's about what you overcome." Wow, there's a new paradigm.

OK, so with that in mind and with some concerns about life that all of us have, what have you overcome or what do you plan to overcome? Can you make a difference in the lives of people, maybe even here, locally? Because, you see, with the right attitude after the wrong experience, greatness really can occur. Think about it...

DBEDT Data

The latest state of Hawai'i data book is available online, and a simple look through some of the charts reveals some fascinating numbers. Now I am not a sociologist, an urbanologist, a futurologist, nor even an ichthyologist, but I do find the facts here to be interesting. Almost 71 percent of the state resides on O'ahu, which is about four percent fewer than resided on O'ahu 15 years ago. Two percent more people now live on the Big Island and in Maui County vs. 15 years ago, while Kaua'i has remained population-steady for the past 15 years.

Out of the total population of 1,268,000 people: 308,000 people listed themselves as Hawaiian or part Hawaiian; 199,000 said they are Japanese; 142,000 Filipino; 292,000 Caucasian; 45,000 Chinese; and 255,000 mixed, but not Hawaiian. Those were the major groups. Talk about a melting pot; talk about a place that stretches out from here to there with all kinds of people in all kinds of places. And to add to the diversity, 162,000 people said they speak Tagalog, Japanese, Chinese, Spanish, or Korean at home—not English.

The sociological conclusion for today is that you better just get along, you better accept, you oughta drop stupid stereotyping; you really need to understand that there are differences and maybe you should even celebrate those differences. If not, we still offer plenty of plane seats, albeit fewer than we had a few months ago, that will easily escort you somewhere else, like maybe a cave or some less tolerant place. So vive la différence, enjoy the human smorgasbord that is Hawai'i, and understand why it's said, "Lucky you live Hawai'i." Think about it...

Stereotyping, even in joke form, has an undercurrent that's ugly—anytime.

October 20, 2008

Mouse House

Nice to see that in the midst of the tough economic times that someone is thinking long-term. Disney's plans to move ahead with a hotel and time-share concept out at Ko Olina will provide a new destination for visitors to ponder as they think of Hawaiʻi, and will also provide about a thousand new jobs. And that's when the resort opens, but there will be plenty of construction work in the next few months.

This will certainly not be a Mickey Mouse operation, with the Disney touch added to the local touches of culture, history, plants, etc. It's yet another Disney experience, right here in our own backyard. And it's not a fairy tale—it's actually going to be built. Too often we hear of projects that then seem to take forever to get going like a West Oahu campus or rapid transit, or projects that take forever to get completed like the elevated highway by the airport or the roadwork on Kapiʻolani, Nimitz, in Kailua, well, just about everywhere.

Most of us know from experience that Disney does things right—yes, they are certainly not "goofy," pardon the pun—so this 830 total units resort with a family emphasis should be a nice addition to the growing number of projects planned on the leeward side. And this one is actually going to become a reality soon, Tinker Bell. Think about it...

Aulani is going strong, but other projects mentioned here...not so much.

November 5, 2008

Time to Rail-y

Rail, rail, the gang's all here. Now that the rapid transit issue has been decided upon by the voters, let's see just how quickly, or slowly, it takes to get the wheels in motion on this huge project. How long before we hear from the many community voices that will be directly impacted, maybe even physically impacted, by the rail system?

Now is the time for civil discussions about land usage, timing, and noise concerns—whether true or untrue. Now is the time to work with the environmentalists and community leaders and residents in affected areas. Now is the time to draw really good models to show people what this will all look like—in their neighborhoods. I suspect all of these items are high on the priority list now that it is full speed ahead, all engines forward. Overcommunication would be a good thing for this project, to ensure that no one is left behind due to lack of understanding or awareness.

Moving forward in general is the easy part; the devil is in the details, as is the inevitable cost of this project. But the more people know, the more they are informed, the more they get the news—good or bad—in advance, the better chance that this project will ride smoothly. Think about it...

And just wait until they drive piles in Māpunapuna and can't find stable bottom at "expected" depths.

Think about it.

November 10, 2008

Barack & Roll

A week ago, history was made in this country. Never before had anyone other than a Caucasian male been chosen to the highest elected position in the land. In one, singular presidential campaign we had a person of mixed race and a female on the ticket. Progress? Most assuredly. Reality? Hard to take for some, but yes, reality...and a local guy to boot. Born, raised, and schooled right here in our islands.

So take a moment now to reflect on just how far we as a nation have come after over 230 years. Put aside your political leanings and realize that the best thing that can happen for this country, for our world, is for Barack Obama to be the best president he can possibly be. Put aside the ridiculous efforts to cast us into camps of red and blue, black and white, lefty and righty, and realize that the most important thing is for this president-elect to be a healer, a realist, and a deliverer of promises. Actually, that wish is no different than the wish we all should have every time a leader is elected, whether it be George W. Bush or Franklin D. Roosevelt.

If you consider yourself a true patriot, an American interested in getting the best for this nation of 50 purple states, don't sit in the corner and pout or cast aspersions. You gotta hope and strive for the best. Because that's what it's all about—what's best for a unified country. Yes, ideologies come into play, but working to heal wounds and solve major problems at home and abroad are priorities. And maybe, just maybe, someone raised and formed with aloha spirit can make a definitive, positive difference in the coming years. It's time to Barack and roll, America. Think about it...

Think about it..

December 1, 2008

Giving Back

It might be tough to decide what to do about gift giving this year, what with the economy and all. It's tough to cut back when you're used to giving annually, but if reality says you must, then you must. Good friends and acquaintances should understand. Maybe giving of your time would be the best and most reasonable gift this year, whether it's to family or friends you simply don't see often enough, or perhaps to a nonprofit or service organization that could really use your help.

And the nice thing about the gift of time and caring, you—the giver—will certainly reap the rewards as much as the gift recipients. And the price is right. It doesn't take much effort to make a few calls or check out local organizations online that can use your help this holiday season—or even after the holiday season ends. And getting involved might take some of the sting out of the economic realities. If we all give back to those we care about and to those we don't even know, it's got to be a good thing, doesn't it?

As this is the annual designated season for giving, for reflecting, for taking the time to care and thank and remember and embrace, now is certainly as good a time as any to figure out what it is you can do with your time, rather than just your wallet. Give from the heart and from your head, and you will certainly feel all the better for it this holiday season 2008. Think about it...

Think about it.

January 5, 2009

Fireworks Don't Work

The name "fireworks" is a misnomer, because we all know that any real, "fire" caused by these "works" can be a great tragedy. I have heard numerous people state that they felt the obnoxious displays were louder and more prevalent this year than in years past. Thanks to Mother Nature, economic factors, and our local fire departments, there were fewer incidents this year than in years past.

Maybe, but watching illegal aerials and hearing almost sonic boom–like blasts for the weeks leading up to New Year's Eve proves, once again, that a lot of work needs to be done to ensure a safer and healthier end to each year here in Hawai'i. Yes, it can be exciting, and yes, some people get a huge adrenaline rush with a plethora of pyrotechnics, but sanity needs to prevail, especially in neighborhood settings and in the weeks leading up to the big date.

We can't depend on rain every year or assume a depressed economy will keep people from loading up on firecrackers, and we can't assume that our local authorities will be able to canvas the entire island chain, citing lawbreakers. For some annual blow up artists, common sense on this issue is something they apparently disavowed a long time ago. Let's just hope that they get a wake-up call on safety and logic before they lose a home, an appendage, or a loved one in the name of over-the-top celebrations and so-called tradition. Think about it...

January 15, 2009

Watt Power?

On December 26 and 27, the power went out on Oʻahu for most people for 12 to 20 hours. It takes a long time (as we have now learned twice in the past two years) to slowly bring the power grid back up to make sure that the whole thing doesn't crash. And yes, we understand that this is an island, and we simply can't borrow power from our next-door neighbor. We don't have one.

But let's hope that real solutions are realized in short order to make sure that if a real emergency hits, that there can be a reasonable expectation of power recovery befitting a state in this country in the 21st century. While I don't pretend to understand the dynamics involved, and I know that there are myriad technical issues involved, we need to know what can be done, what it will cost, and how fast it can be built or installed for reasonable decisions to be made about viability and value.

We also need to make sure that officials provide clear and regularly updated information to radio and television stations—the major conduits to a confused and uncertain public. How about guaranteed updates every half hour, even if there is nothing new, because people deserve to know? Anecdotal call-ins can help ease or add to the tension, but well-coordinated calls from people in the know at frequent intervals sure would have helped. HECO deserves credit for having an on-site spokesperson at one designated radio location, but information needs to get passed along quickly, as many stations used generators to stay on-air and keep people informed. Plus, the Neighbor Islands had radio and TV coverage throughout those darkened hours on Oʻahu. Hopefully, bright solutions will come out of this relatively minor rehearsal. Think about it...

"Hopefully, bright solutions will come out of this relatively minor rehearsal." Frankly, we are 11 years farther down the road, and emergency communications between government entities and mass media (TV, radio) remain a concern. Twitter is not a solution.

It Starts at Home

Yet another ranking has been released suggesting that Hawai'i is still near the bottom when it comes to test scores on a key exam: the SAT. Conversely, to show how unclear this picture might be, Hawai'i did score better than the national average on the comparable ACT test, which puts us in the middle of the national pack. But let's get to the bottom line, beyond rationale about resources, infrastructure, and unique circumstances, all of which have some merit.

When it comes to kids and their thirst for learning, it all starts at home. Parents who think of schools and teachers as surrogate babysitters miss the opportunity to provide their kids with necessary motivation and incentive to succeed. Parents who don't get involved or who are not genuinely interested—even for 10 minutes a day over dinner or while sitting around at night—deprive themselves and their keiki of a golden opportunity to be achievers, role models, or difference makers.

A great teacher talking to a classroom of disinterested kids is at a huge disadvantage. A child who does not see the value in learning and in being a productive member of a school environment is, unfortunately, making bad, youthful decisions that might very well last a lifetime. Yes, some of our schools and teachers need to do a better job. So do some of our parents. Think about it...

Mister Twister

The term "hero" is used too often in our world these days. To me, a heroic act is when someone shows great courage and goes out of his or her way and even puts themselves in harm's way. Ask a serviceman, a fireman, a policeman, or even an astronaut if what they do in the course of their job requirement is heroic and they would most certainly tell you no. Ask the trained personnel involved in emergencies from 9/11 to landing a plane in the Hudson River if their necessary actions constitute heroism and most if not all would tell you no.

But when a tornado touched down in Kapolei last Wednesday an assistant golf pro helped secure a panicked golfer as the tornado literally tried to pry her from her golf cart and the word "hero" seemed to be most appropriate. Going above and beyond and entering into a funnel cloud...that's almost mythical in its very nature. After instructing coworkers to get inside Neil Bernard made that instantaneous decision that heroes have to make—do I stay or do I go? And he went. And he helped. And he was tossed against a wall and suffered head and neck injuries. He had seen hurricanes in Samoa but now he was truly in the eye of the storm and he reacted in a way that perhaps saved lives and certainly prevented injuries.

Without much forethought in a matter of seconds, because one never knows when the time may come to act heroically, this young man became an amazing story. And these days an uplifting incident like this one—uplifting in more ways than one—certainly makes you feel good. Think about it...

Think about it.

Fee, Please

Become self-sufficient, UH Athletics Department! Oh, by the way, you get no parking revenue in the lower campus parking lot for all of your events, you get no concessions revenue or parking revenue at Aloha Stadium, you get minimal licensing royalties and no merchandising revenue from clothing sales on campus, and while the university is raising tuition, the athletics department does not get tuition waivers, which some other schools' athletic departments do get. And, UH is the only school in the WAC that doesn't impose a student athletic fee.

Well the time has come. Yes, the student senate has said, "No thank you," again to the thought of imposing an annual athletics fee, but that's no shock. No one chooses to see taxes raised, rent raised, food prices raised, but sometimes it happens. Ask any student or parent if they would like to see tuition raised; as a matter of fact, most would probably vote to pay no tuition at all. But if we are to keep up with at least the other schools in the WAC, and faced with the realities of tough economic times for fans and sponsors alike, now seems like a really good time to charge full-time UH students $100 a year or so. That $2 per week per student would add over $2 million to the athletic department coffers annually, while at the same time provide students with some free tickets if they want.

It's never a good time to raise prices or increase fees, but this is one area that should be addressed now for the department's sake, and for the sake of the student athletes who provide so much for the university. It's all part of the price to remain competitive and to help provide a more complete student experience, because athletes, just like laboratory lovers and library denizens, are part of the essence of a university. Think about it...

UH should impose an additional $50 student fee per semester in 2020, to approach parity with its brethren in the Big West and Mountain West conferences.

April 1, 2009

Superferry Supernova

Superman was impervious to bullets and bombs as he went about his business. Super glue is supposed to be the greatest bonding product of all time—it's not. The Super Bowl is the ultimate championship of US football. The list of super-lative items goes on and on. But what of the Superferry? Did it not live up to its expectations as an alternative mode of transport? It did, providing a quality service, helping businesses, consumers, charities, and even keeping its extremities away from sea life during its short tenure here.

What Superferry couldn't do in the long haul was rely on the very same people who assured it that it would be able to operate while an Environmental Impact Statement was being undertaken. Sure, there are plenty who will say, "I told you so," that the EIS should have been properly completed before the ship set sail. But the Superferry was assured that they would have smooth sailing by the top branches of our state government, and now the state Supreme Court has said, "Not so fast." The legislation that was invalidated means we might not see this ship sail again, at least not in our waters, and the business ripples are just beginning to affect those who had grown accustomed to this burgeoning enterprise.

So while we still have really big ships plowing between islands and through our ocean whose environmental impact probably has greater day-to-day impact than the Superferry did, we have managed to dock this effort because the adults in charge could not get it right in the first place, at whatever level you want to place blame. And perhaps even sadder, it's not a shock to many longtime locals. Think about it...

Good news! The Superferry (Alaka'i) still runs in the summertime— between Nova Scotia and Portland, Maine.

When Les is More

I first met Les Keiter back in the late 1960s. Actually, it was a one-way meeting via the TV screen, as I sat there watching him perform his Philadelphia TV sports anchor job while I visited my cousins in Cherry Hill, New Jersey. Les always grabbed my attention through his delivery of baseball scores, highlights, and standings, even as a kid. That voice, that delivery, that passion.

My first full-time job here in June of 1977 included coming face-to-face with Les. He was the sports guru at Channel 2, and I was the wide-eyed "kid" who handled public relations for Hawai'i's new, pro soccer team—Team Hawaii. He always greeted me in a festive manner, and I cherished that he called me "the kid." Of course, to Les, everyone was the kid—an endearing term, for he treated everyone fairly and with respect, and he provided me with a positive rush of adrenaline to my evolving self-esteem system. And, he was one of the few sports guys who actually took a regular interest in accepting the fledgling pro soccer venture back then.

Over the years, I would see Les at UH sporting events at the Stan Sheriff Center, at Aloha Stadium, and at Quarterback Club luncheons. He never changed—always up, always interested, always present. He made me feel a sense of self-worth at age 21 just by his ingratiating style as a mentor, and I will always have a soft spot in my heart and soul for him...in a "general" way. Aloha, Les. Think about it...

May 27, 2009

Military Salute

We are coming to the end of Military Appreciation Month this weekend, and whether or not you are a big fan of our specific war efforts right now, this month represents a moment for all of us to be more cognizant of our military, its efforts, and provide a timely moment to say thanks. That's all, just a simple thank you to a passing woman or man in military dress would be a thoughtful sign that you care about and appreciate those who defend your rights aboard, every day.

What else can you do? Send an email or letters of thanks, send a care package overseas, fly the flag in your yard or at work, wear a wristband showing support. There are lots of ways to show your appreciation for the valiant efforts of these people who diligently carry out their assigned duties both here in Hawai'i and wherever they are called, sometimes at a moment's notice, and often times, in harm's way.

That guy you just passed in the mall...he might have had two or three tours of duty already. That woman having a meal at the restaurant table next to you...she might be about to leave for an assignment overseas. I know we're all taught not to talk to strangers, but a simple "Thanks for all you do," might go a long way, especially coming from a complete stranger. It's Military Appreciation Month for a few more days—and you can do your part. Think about it...

Think about it.

June 1, 2009

Neighborhood Bored

What if they held an election and no one showed up? What if they held an election and no one ran? Well, it's not quite that bad, but the recent turnout, for the neighborhood board elections indicated that something's wrong in the big city. Only six percent of eligible voters bothered to transmit their votes electronically or by phone, which were the only ways to vote this time around.

One of the reasons for the low turnout by voters was the incredibly low turnout of candidates. Over 60 percent of the areas had uncontested races, which means if mommy voted for you, you're in! This is no way meant to condemn the intent of these community boards, nor is it meant to impugn the fine people who take the time to volunteer and run for these offices. I don't think people realize just exactly what it is that neighborhood board members do, or why this grassroots effort has a value to communities and neighborhoods.

Sure, hackers might get involved, just like voter fraud is always a possibility at polling places. As they used to say in Chicago and New Orleans, "Vote early and vote often." To really get people to vote, the system might not matter so much as the message being sent—get the people interested, involved, and to the point where they see the value of their vote, and they are more likely to show up online, on the phone, or at polls. Think about it...

Think about it.

June 22, 2009

Kim Gee

An old truism in child-rearing says don't threaten your child with a punishment unless you plan to follow through. No follow-through, no repercussion for unacceptable deeds, no lesson learned. Taking this concept to the political realities of 2009, we have a country, North Korea, which seems to be threatened with sanctions and such time and time again by the international community. It's hard to cut off a country that pretty much seems to exist in its own world by cutting itself off, but the stakes just got a wee bit higher as reports indicate that North Korea just may be preparing to fire a missile in our direction sometime early next month.

While little can be said by military officials in this country, you can be sure that our wary eyes on this habitual defier just got a little bit more focused. The Japanese newspaper that reported the story said that the missile would not be able to reach our islands, but the mere fact that this report might have some credence certainly means that everyone—from China to Russia to Japan to the US—has to do a better job of ensuring that this xenophobic nation does not become more than just a mysterious nuisance.

Relationships with North Korea, strained at best for many, many years, have now taken a greater urgency with reports of inevitable nuclear capabilities and missiles capable of reaching further destinations—perhaps even the West Coast of this country in a few years. This is not a simple game with a simple answer, but the international community must do a better job in difficult times to help ensure that we all feel a bit safer. Think about it...

Think about it.

Big Time Little League

Another Waipio Little League team did our state proud last week in Williamsport, Pennsylvania. The recent run of successful Hawai'i teams in this sport and age group is incredible, but it shouldn't come as a complete surprise. After all, the network of support for our keiki in organized sports is perhaps unsurpassed just about anywhere else, and the calm displayed by these kids and their coaches throughout the trials and tribulations in front of bright lights, thousands of fans, and really big TV cameras showed solid island-style demeanor—cool and focused.

People often talk about the so-called "aloha" lifestyle, and it's one of the vital attributes that makes these islands stand apart from many other destinations for visitors. So when we have a chance to share that spirit—even through our youngest ambassadors—it reflects well on everybody here.

From the Sugar Bowl to NCAA volleyball tournaments to Little League to soccer and golf events, Hawai'i's sporting participants and their traveling fans are considered a class act, and that's a nice nod these days where too often manners take a back seat to uncontrolled emotions and embarrassing outbursts. Nice job kids, in more ways than perhaps you can realize at the tender age of 12. Think about it…

Add in a third, O'ahu-based team Little League championship title in 2018, plus a strong run by a Maui team in Williamsport in 2019, and the beat goes on for Hawai'i youth baseball.

Think about it..

Helping Hand-out

My state senator showed up at my door on Saturday afternoon. Dressed plainly, she handed me a brochure and asked if there was anything that she could help me with. I said, "No, thanks," and thanked her for stopping by. I read through the brochure and gained a little better insight into her thinking and her past; in fact, I might just vote for her based on her positions, track record, and the fact that she is canvassing and asking questions on a hot Saturday in a most unassuming way.

Now this is not the ultimate rationale for voting for or against somebody, but it sure made a lot better impression on me than having a bunch of people standing on the roadway with insincere smiles trying to distract me from the job at hand—driving in stop-and-go traffic every morning. We need more people who are involved in their communities at the grassroots level, who really have their constituents' best interests at hand and prove it, literally walking the walk, not just talking or waving.

What we don't need are career politicians, those who simply run every couple of years to maintain a job and maintain the status quo. What we don't need are people in government providing lip service about being pro education, pro job creation, and/or pro-environment who really just want to stay employed, putting in years of so-called service, even if it means rowing in the same boat with people and ideas they don't think are right. We need fighters, believers, and change masters in office, not "perfunctionaries" most interested in their own health benefits and retirement plans. Is anybody listening? Think about it…

Can you say "term limits"? Career politicians were never in the forefathers' plan.

May 30, 2011

Defenseless

I have been a bit puzzled over the past few weeks as I've noticed more and more of those Defend Hawaii T-shirts with an assault rifle on the front. I am well aware of the emotional issues regarding sovereignty, preserving culture, and indigenous people's rights, but does a shirt with a weapon of mass destruction on the front really make a necessary statement or is it trying to signify that we are under attack from who knows whom?

One blog I saw suggested that the Defend Hawaii concept is about preserving the aloha spirit so unique and special to these islands. And that's a reasonable and noble idea. But when do an AK-47 and the word "aloha" ever fit into the same sentence, let alone argument?

Do you want to know how Hawai'i is being properly "defended"? When a record number of students (15) graduate from the UH law school with a Native Hawaiian Law Certificate. When cultural programs celebrating local customs and lifestyle flourish and attract more interest from people here and abroad. When Native Hawaiian businesses grow and thrive and Native Hawaiians win positions of power through elected offices. When more students graduate from our schools and are better educated to ensure that they have more chances for success in life on a cluster of islands with no neighbors for 2,500 miles. When people from over 90 countries watch the Merrie Monarch Festival internet streaming and learn more about the ancient and beautiful art of hula.

That's how we defend Hawai'i, support Hawai'i, and showcase Hawai'i. That's how we move forward, protect ourselves, and keep vibrant that which is sacred as we humbly show our pride. That's how we keep this melting pot from boiling over, even in tough times. Think about it…

August 29, 2011

Déjà Whew

Here we go again...maybe. The Department of Business, Economic Development & Tourism's latest economic projections have been revised downwards from bigger growth projections proffered in May in the areas of jobs and tourism numbers. The new report suggests that while we might still see growth in the near future in those vital areas, the optimism has faded somewhat due, in part, to the continued lethargy of the US and Japanese economies in general.

DBEDT director Richard Lim said, "We must continue to shift Hawai'i's economy to a more independent and sustainable foundation." Sound familiar? It should, as it's the same story that's been told to us by economists, business moguls, professors, and politicians for at least the past 30 years locally. But coming to grips with how to become more self-sufficient and less dependent on the volatile real world outside of Hawai'i has always been the real question.

Fifty years ago, sugar, pineapple, and seemingly unique agricultural opportunities were seen as great salvations for our economy; not so today. Tourism has been the mainstay of our economic engine for decades, but it ebbs and flows based on world events and issues that are completely out of our control. Military spending is a vital piece of our economy, helped in no small part by the efforts over the years of our senators and representatives in Washington, DC, and by world events where Hawai'i is seen as well positioned. But what's next? What can we do to better ensure our economic survival and self-sufficiency in the economic rollercoaster that is the 21st century? Those are billion-dollar answers that we need to keep searching for. Think about it...

It's 2020. Do we have 20/20 vision on our future beyond 2020, or even glasses that help us to see our future opportunities beyond tourism? We need some farsightedness followed by action.

Time Waits for No One

I was sitting in traffic the other day (ah yes, the old back-to-school mambo) and noticed a brand-new car that had the temporary license plate. The only trouble was that the date on the plate was 9/31/11. You see, September only has 30 days, so this car has a date that simply doesn't exist in our current understanding of time. And I thought to myself, Wouldn't it be cool if we could determine time, and not be constricted by the mandates of the universe as we know it.

And then someone honked and I moved six inches closer to my destination. But, as the Rolling Stones once beautifully lamented, "Time waits for no one, and it won't wait for me." Only you can determine your control over time, or its control over you. Only you can determine how much time you want to spend in the various areas of your life—recreation, personal, business, etc. When someone says, "I didn't have time," what that means in reality is that everything that they had to do or chose to do precluded them from dealing with whatever it is you were asking for or expecting.

The bottom line is we're all busy, we're all rushing, we're all caught in traffic, or have too many emails to deal with, or have to rush to pick up the kids from soccer practice or have to get off one more tweet. Don't let time get away from you without truly spending some real quality time where you want to spend it. Because some day, you really won't have any more time, and you'll wonder where it all went. And no one ever lay on his or her deathbed and said, "Darn, I wish I'd have spent more time in the office." Think about it...

Stop Kidding Around

My good friend Peter just wrote a letter to the speaker of the House of Representatives and to the president of the Senate. You can find that letter in the editorial section of our K5 website. In it, he asks for the different factions to get together and do something constructive, such as working toward a common goal of getting this country back on track. In his letter, he suggests that Congress take a look at the collaborative work going on in his kid's elementary school, where respectful disagreement leads to learning, compromising, collaborating, and getting things done.

He also suggests rearranging the seats in the austere legislative branches from time to time, much like they do in his kid's classes on Maui. This encourages helping one another out, having an open mind, and keeps all the like-minded or like-acting people from hanging together, as that often causes cliques, whispering, and disruption. Maybe this suggestion would work in our own legislature, though there really aren't two diverse sides since our legislative branches are not split up evenly. But maybe listening to disparate points of view, or getting everyone in a room at the same time would help us solve some of our problems—on labor issues, on fiduciary responsibility and the hard cuts that must be made, on long-term decisions for the betterment of the state under trying conditions.

Sending a message to the masses via congressional reconciliation that the adults really are willing to work together—and not just playing to a constituent base or trying to get reelected—would be a great lesson for our kids. Or maybe this time, as Peter suggests, the kids can teach the adults how to act and maybe get things done for the good of us all. Think about it...

Think about it.

February 13, 2012

Ship to Shore

There was a great story last week about the three visitors from Canada who were rescued from the sea by a container ship that was in the area and heeded the SOS call. Many people involved did smart and even brave things to make this sea tale a happy one. The huge Horizon ship came to the rescue; the brothers in the ailing sailboat used satellite phones, strobes, and life vests; and little West James held up hope and his head until they all got pulled on deck.

And as soon as the story broke, with the ship's captain confirming just how merciless the sea was that night, you could hear the mad scramble of agents, book writers, movie honchos, and magazine editors heading over here to grab a piece of the action. A movie for the ages! A cover story that might preempt a celebrity divorce or meltdown! Nine-year-old West James's diary—the mobile app, coming soon to your phone! Saga at sea— the imperfect storm, sharks lurking and licking their chops! You know the hyperbole.

Wouldn't it be nice if once in a while, heroic efforts and good stories that arise from bad circumstances had their day in the sun, and then quietly faded off into the sunset? Is it possible that this lucky threesome will go back home to Alberta and resume normal day-to-day lives and recount the story a few hundred times to curious friends and neighbors. Or have we reached the point where everyone who does anything of note, good or bad, is made a celebrity? The best news is that these guys made the local and international news by avoiding what could have been a tragedy. Can we possibly just let it go at that? Think about it…

Good news: No movie or book—yet. But the addiction to feeding social media and digital news engines 24/7 means nothing stays quiet for long, or lasts for long.

Think about it.

February 16, 2012

A Gift That Keeps On Giving

While the state House deferred a bill last week that might have allowed for lawmakers to accept more gifts from possible influencers, we shouldn't kid ourselves into thinking that lawmakers are still not influenced by lobbyists and campaign contributors. Ethics have to do with moral principles, social values, and professional standards, and those things should not be pliable for anybody, let alone elected officials.

At the same time, to suggest that human beings are not going to be influenced by people and/or industries that come in contact with them based on relationships, past or present, is silly. What we can expect is that our elected officials will make their decisions that are based on what is best for the people of Hawai'i, the voters, their constituent base. At the end of the day, we all have to first answer to ourselves first when we make decisions that call our integrity or our ethics into question. If you can lie and deceive yourself, then obviously you will feel free to do the same to others, and you should not be allowed to serve in public office. The voters will hopefully make that call, and we've seen instances of transgressions and bad judgment costing local politicians over the years…as it should be. No one's perfect, but we do expect something closer to perfection from people in powerful positions, including politicians. They ask for our support and trust, which they must continually earn and then cherish.

In 1989, Spike Lee directed a movie called Do the Right Thing. You might forget the movie, but just think about the title's simple concept. If you have a hard time knowing what is the right thing and you are an elected official, there are channels for you to check things out, before you might do the wrong thing. Issues regarding ethics and professional standards are not always black and white, but a little self-assessment and self-reflection by those in power is a good thing, regardless of what bills may be pushed forward related to gifts and ethics. Think about it…

Sorry, reality suggests that a part-time legislature (and thus a part-time job for most legislators) ensures constant conflicts of interest and ethical quandaries, whereby the dark side of human nature (greed, self-preservation) comes into play.

Paradise Revisited

It's a constant struggle in paradise. Development in Kailua town and how it will affect the small town feel there. Koloa Camp property on Kaua'i and the ramifications of development. Commercial activity at beaches in Hale'iwa, Kailua, and elsewhere, and the concern of potentially ruining what is so special for so many. Hāmākua rezoning for housing, high-rises in Kaka'ako, Superferry, H-3, a rail alternative for leeward O'ahu...the list goes on and on.

This is not a market that readily embraces change, and sometimes that's a good thing. We like a lot of the things that make our small niches of Hawai'i unique, special, and relatively unchanged from year to year, decade to decade. And it's great when conversations are had amongst those involved in proposing changes and those affected by changes. It's the way a civil society is supposed to be run. But keep in mind that we only have so much room for a growing population base here that will continue to require or at least request changes that might make some lives better or at least happier. More people, more traffic, more stress on services, more spreading out—it is part of Hawai'i, like it or not, just like it is in other areas that are better equipped to handle urban sprawl simply due to their size.

The Kuhio Grill, Coco's, Arakawa's, and Liberty House are all gone. So are most of the sugarcane, pineapple, and dairy farms of yesteryear. We cherish our nostalgia and try to hold on to those things we believe in or remember dearly, while at the same time sadly realize that maybe nothing is forever, including landmarks and landscapes. You can replace and remove, you can modernize and rationalize, but you can't easily erase memories, and sometimes, in some cases and somewhere down the line, that's all we're going to have. Think about it...

Think about it.

March 29, 2012

Writing Wrongs

In the March issue of HONOLULU Magazine, there is a nice tribute to the late great writer John Heckathorn, who tragically and suddenly passed away three months ago. Heckathorn was a character, and I mean that in the finest way. He was also a connoisseur of food who could make your mouth water by just reading his stories about delicious discoveries. But he was also a provocative author on just about any subject area he dabbled in.

The HONOLULU Magazine piece this month offered us pūpū from John—bits and paragraphs from many great articles that Heckathorn wrote. One piece really struck home for me. In a 2003 article, he mentioned that he had now interviewed three Hawaiʻi governors, going back to 1987, and he mentioned, in 2003, that while talking to each interviewee/governor over the years, he "...was struck by how similar many of the themes were. The economy. The failings of the public schools. The inefficiency of state government. The need to settle the ceded lands questions and find justice for Hawaiians."

And here we are in 2012, fully nine years after his last governor chat and 25 years since John's first gubernatorial interview and gosh darn, it sure seems like those same topics and issues are, as yet, unresolved in just about every area: the economy, public schools, state government, justice for Hawaiians, land issues. While the leaders have changed over the years, the vicious syndrome of stasis remains here in far too many areas. John Heckathorn was a clever, upbeat, worldly writer who didn't get to see these issues resolved. Will we? Think about it...

"Will we" (see these issues resolved)? Uh, still not yet...

April 26, 2012

Lama Logic

For those who were lucky enough to attend, the Dalai Lama most assuredly made quite an impression when he spoke here recently. His messages of tolerance, happiness, respectfulness, empathy, and accountability actually don't sound that far off from our vaunted value of living aloha.

So why is it so difficult? Why has human discourse become so inhumane, so personal, so attacking, so vitriolic? Well, there's ego, pride, self-assuredness, insecurity, desire for power and control, and about 20 other human foibles that prevent us from all simply getting along. When people think they are so right in their opinions and when people believe they are justified to prove they are right with might, bad things happen; check the history books.

The arrogance of people in power under the cloak of supposed religious or political superiority is astounding and troubling. The fact that some of the very same people who would dare to impose rigid dogmas and absolutisms on how we should live our lives are people who actually cheat on their taxes, cheat at golf, cheat on their wives, and/or cheat in the workplace is baffling. How about if more people who adhere to this quote from the Dalai Lama: "Our prime purpose in this life is to help others. And if you can't help them, at least don't hurt them." Simple, straightforward, practical, and yet apparently so very hard for so many. But it's a good goal, even in Hawai'i. Think about it…

Think about it...

April 30, 2012

Cuts Without Clues

Over and over, you hear uninformed people talk about the need to cut government, to keep government out of our lives, just leave us alone. A simple thought that assumes an enlightened and capable citizenry living without the onerous burden of Big Brother imposing sanctions on people's lives or reaching deeper into their pockets. OK, I get it, but at what price? Dig one inch below the surface of that simplistic concept, and where are you?

Reduce government? Really? Fewer supplies and repairs for our public schools? Less attention focused on our crumbling roads and infrastructure? Fewer agencies available to help out during catastrophic natural disasters? Fewer firefighters and police officers? Fewer agriculture inspectors in Hawai'i already means we have fewer eyes making sure we keep out brown tree snakes, Central African beetles, infectious mosquitoes, and other malicious pests. How about proposing some cutbacks in government services that would really help reduce our deficit by a significant amount? Sounds great, doesn't it? Well, most economists of any political bent will tell you that the biggest cuts necessary to have a real lasting impact on mitigating our debt would have to come via slashing defense spending, Social Security, Medicare and/or Medicaid. Now, who wants to make that call? Surely no politician who wants to be reelected will dare touch those areas.

Yes, less government sounds great. Bureaucrats tend to get in the way and entrepreneurs need not apply. But until someone can logically explain how to make this all work with real cost cutting but without long-term implications that no one wants to deal with, it's all just lip service and generic posturing in Hawai'i and nationally. It makes for good sound bites and water cooler chatter, but it's really just vacuous vamping without details. Think about it…

OK, so maybe less government isn't coming soon, but how about better, more efficient, more proactive government? Is that unfathomable, too?

May 3, 2012

Facebunk

I went to a movie last week and was perturbed by the cell phones that stayed on, even as the movie began and as some self-absorbed individual got a hugely important text midway through the feature. I went to a meeting last week and watched as numerous people thought they were being subtle as they checked their Crackberries during the meeting while others spoke to the group. They could have picked boogers and been more subtle than trying to glance down under the table for that all-important missive that simply couldn't wait an hour. At a restaurant the other night, I noticed at another table a lovely couple that was completely oblivious to one another due to the incessant texting going on...how romantic and special that evening must have been.

I guess we have devolved as a species into a rather rude, hyperactive, always connected, always distracted group just dying to know what we might be missing every 30 seconds. Which I guess makes us not much different from squirrels or mongeese, nervously on the watch to see what's going on around us. I know there are major sociological implications in this incessant tweeting, texting, and social networking, and I can't help but wonder if it's making people in Hawai'i a bit more numb and detached. Hawai'i's people are arguably the nicest people anywhere, to generalize, but you have to wonder about our sometimes casual lifestyles being so drastically impacted by little devices that require so much time and attention, at what expense?

Yes, all those portable devices have a purpose, but if we are really in charge, then we should have the self-confidence, self-restraint, and self-control to sometimes simply turn the things off—not on silent, but off. We have had enough pedestrian incidents of late, so we shouldn't have to worry about Timmy getting nailed in an intersection by a wayward vehicle because he was too busy sending his dinner plans to a Facebook page, should we? Think about it...

The tech addiction is surely worse than ever, for all age groups. Likes, thumbs up, followers, tags—are we really becoming herds of sheep? Bah! Take a tech break.

Think about it.

May 28, 2012

Time for Term Limits?

One of the many reasons that things often don't get done during legislative sessions is the fact that most legislators, both local and national, are very careful not to alienate their core constituent base because if they anger their base supporters they might be out of a job next time around. So, safety prevails, even at the expense of making bold and necessary changes some times. Term limits were more the norm in this country 225 years ago, and the push surfaced again about 30 years ago, but interest in enacting such limits has died down of late. US House and Senate incumbents, when they run again, are reelected about 95 percent of the time. That's stunning.

Proponents for term limits argue that elected officials get too comfortable with special interests, lose sight of what's going on in the streets back home, lack fresh ideas, and see the position as a presumed seat for as long as they want it. Those against term limits say limits discount experience and might keep good people from going after the jobs. Well, the US Congress currently sports a 90 percent disapproval rating, so apparently a lot of American voters think something's wrong or has got to change. And what about the US Supreme Court, which is a job that lasts "during good behavior," as it is written, which can be a lifetime.

Oliver Wendell Holmes Jr. and John Paul Stevens retired as Supremes at age 90. Should the biggest decisions in this country really be made by people who might not be at the top of their game and simply can't see a reason to step aside? It's food for thought. Thomas Jefferson was a big fan of term limits, and many people thought and think he was a pretty sharp guy. Like standing water, perhaps elected and appointed decision makers get stagnant and need to be flushed out with some fresh water over time. It's not an insult to suggest as much, just some subjective food for thought.

About 15 of our state legislatures have some form of term limits. The basic premise is do your best work, and then move on and let someone else move in. We don't feel that way in Hawai'i. We are champions of protecting the status quo in far too many ways and places, starting with the legislature. Maybe now is the time to revisit this concept at home and in Washington, DC. Maybe the people should decide, since it's their country after all. Think about it…

Yes, term limits at many levels of officialdom make sense. Still.

Think about it

July 5, 2012

Making Every Second Count

You may have missed it, hopefully not. Last Saturday at 2 p.m. local time the international keepers of time on this planet added one second to the official clock. Yes, one second. It seems that the earth rotates on its axis now about two milliseconds slower than it did 100 years ago; yes, Mother Earth is slowing down and—dare I say it—becoming an old lady, I guess. Old man time, meet old lady earth. So the timekeepers add a second every once in a while to ensure that the sun hits its highest point at exactly noon.

But the big question is: Did you take advantage? We all know people locally who say, "Oh, if I only had more time"…well, now you've got it. Yes, it might seem small, one second added every few years, but think of the possibilities. More time to do those things you want to do; less rushing around; more focus; more quality time; less time wasted on excuses, tweeting, texting, and emails, which probably take up way too much time. And it is your time. And no one ever lay on his or her deathbed, surrounded by loved ones, and said, "You know, I just wish I'd spent more time at the office."

So maybe we don't need atomic clock watchers to help us do a better job of personal timekeeping. Maybe we should realize that we do control our own time and our choices of what we do with that time. We do decide what we do and what we deem too important to miss. And if you find yourself regretting what it is that you don't do, who it is that you don't see, and maybe even where you don't go, then maybe it's time to fix your watch…literally. Think about it.

Fix your watch—unless it's reminding you about how many steps you've taken, today's news tidbits, who just called and described his/ her lunch to you, and so forth. In that case, toss your watch.

July 16, 2012

Political Speak 101

As we wind our way through televised debates, now is a good time for a two-part "Think About It..." to help you better understand or question the sometimes inane clichés and expressions used by local and national politicians as the campaign season heats up. When a candidate says, "to be frank," we understand—sometimes you are Frank, sometimes you are Sally, sometimes you are Kimo—whatever it takes to make your point. Likewise, "to be honest" is a good one—oh, you mean sometimes you are not honest? Oh for shame.

Many candidates promise to "hit the ground running," although you might get hurt with the fall and sometimes simple walking seems to be a problem with impasses and the incessant lack of resolutions within the system. Since when does politics and decision-making ever move along quickly? Here's another good one: "We are at a critical point." Oh, I see, last year and 1995 and 1987 were not critical points, but now we really need to get serious...thanks for the heads-up. And I love when we are told that we can no longer afford "politics as usual." Really, so now we are all going to band together with the various disparate parties and make joint decisions for the benefit of the human race? Now that would be something. Until then, it really is politics as usual—assuaging egos, gaining power and control, ensuring reelection.

And do question when someone wants to "grow the economy" or "break the gridlock," overused terms for sure. Really now, is there someone left who doesn't want to grow the economy or break the gridlock? More on this later this week, but for now, feel free to "think about it..."

Political Speak 201

We continue tonight to discuss the various terms and redundant, yet useless expressions used by so many locally and elsewhere who really do want our vote. When a politician says, "...and I am passionate," would we want it any other way? Of course, passion sometimes blocks logical thought, so please don't get too passionate and lose control.

How about when politicos talk about "the fact of the matter"; as opposed to what—the lies of the matter or the facts of the anti-matter? We expect the facts and plain speak when we pick our leaders, but we don't get it often enough as candidate pander to special interests, and work hardest at getting reelected.

And when you hear the pledge about "doing more with less," please understand that most of us in the private sector have been doing just that for years—at work and at home, as the economy our politicians have toyed with has not moved very far very fast in the past few years. As I mentioned on Monday, when you hear that we can't afford to see "politics as usual" going forward, does that mean that we're going to have a revolution or rebellion? Because short of that, it sure seems like we will have politics as usual, as distasteful as that has become in the polarized world of Washington, DC. "Fiscal responsibility"—no, we prefer to always be on the edge of default or bankruptcy, worrying about our futures. How about showing some physical responsibility—where you actually do the "heavy lifting" and get things done with compromise and rational thinking, even if it might aggravate some donors?

And to help our keiki and the future of our state, we are told that can't keep "kicking the can down the road." Obviously, kicking a can is not good for the environment and can cause lockjaw if the can is rusty and you get jabbed, so let's stop kicking and starting properly disposing of cans and tired, vacuous, redundant, undeliverable promises and vapid expressions, please. Think about it...

The 2020 elections are coming up. Here we go again!

August 27, 2012

The Wonder of It All

The best (or worst) reality show of late has been the debacle at UH regarding the athletics director situation and the investigation of the non–Stevie Wonder concert. Rather than simply speculate about who did what when, I thought I might put things in context through some Stevie Wonder song titles, and since Mr. Wonder is obviously not going to be serenading us soon, this will have to do for now.

"Signed, Sealed, Delivered I'm Yours"—well, we know that certainly wasn't the case in this event on many levels. Smart people tried to be entrepreneurial to help UH. It didn't work out. "I Wish"—yes, I wish and we all wish this thing hadn't occurred, but it left an opening for obfuscation as a good man, Jim Donovan, was moved aside. "Master Blaster (Jammin')"—the barbs have been coming in droves, deservingly so, from the media, fans, supporters, legislators, and Hawai'i taxpayers—that would be just about everyone who cares or lives here.

"Uptight (Everything's Alright)"—lots of angst and uncertainty in many uptight people in top positions of power trying to figure out what to do or how to avoid doing things. It's also tough to do a top job when outside influencers have too much say. "You Haven't Done Nothin'"—that's what they finally told Jim Donovan about the Wonder blunder, but please step aside anyway. "Don't You Worry 'Bout a Thing"—that's what they're telling us now—new AD to be hired, new controls in place, everything will be just fine; yeh, but the same old system and backroom politics. As Stevie would have said, "Very superstitious, writing's on the wall." Think about it…

Sadly, Stevie still hasn't performed here since his name was used in vain, and the Stan Sheriff Center is still not being used for concert events in the 120-day, mostly unused window between April 15 and August 15 annually.

September 6, 2012

(Heroically) Just Doing the Job

There was a great story early last week about Maui police officers helping residents escape a home fire in Kahului. The alert actions of Officer Slonim and his compatriots who arrived shortly after Slonim first witnessed the smoke in the early morning hours of Monday, August 27 saved lives. One of the great moments of this story, beyond the obvious saving of lives, is what rookie officer Slonim told the media, and I quote, "I was just doing my job. Nothing extraordinary, just my job. I just did what I had to do with my partners."

Too often we quickly label people "heroes" for doing things that we find extraordinary, while the people who perform these seemingly heroic tasks deflect the credit and acknowledge that they knew the job was dangerous when they took it. Astronauts are not heroes, they are highly skilled, adventuresome people doing really meticulous and dangerous work. Police officers and firefighters have very tough jobs, by definition, and from time to time they do incredible things in the line of duty. But ask any of them if they are heroes, and their understanding of the term would indicate that no, they are not heroes, they're just well-trained working men and women going about their jobs.

The dictionary definition of "hero" includes showing great courage, achievement, ability, or strength. But when your job definition also includes those traits, along with humility, you are satisfied by knowing that you do what you need to do to get the job done. So hats off to Maui police officers Slonim, Honda, and Takayama for their brave actions last week. They may be role models and epitomize the best of their profession, but we won't call them heroes. Think about it…

Think about it.

September 13, 2012

Reading is Right

Last week I was fortunate enough to have the opportunity to read to and talk to kids again at Moanalua Middle School during their annual Extreme Reading Kickoff event. The reading program at MMS is well run and well coordinated by passionate teachers and administrators, and this year's focus is on visualization. Visualization asks kids to open up their minds to really see what is being read to them or by them.

One of the many problems of our techno-crazed society today is that a new generation of kids is growing up so wired and so connected that they are not using certain parts of their brain that reading and visualizing help to stimulate. And with disuse comes atrophy, making it harder to pick up and learn new ideas as the years go on. Much like the game of chess forces the player to think a few moves ahead, visualizing while reading allows creative readers to look ahead as to what might be coming up. Reading can improve creativity, relieve stress, teach kids to focus, and helps to remove them, at least for a while, from the sensory overload of electronic contraptions, including TV. Can your kids turn of their cell phone or wireless device for a few hours without sweating or going into spasms? Can you?

Whether it's a book, a magazine, an intriguing website, a fun story— whatever the vehicle may be, take the time to encourage your kids to read, and let them know that reading helps the brain just like jogging and nutritional food help the body. Another way to look at it is, the more stuff you know and store in your brain, the more interested you may be in the world and the more interesting you may be to others, which sure helps as you grow older and search for jobs, significant others, and maybe even the meaning of life. Hook a kid on reading today, and everyone wins. Think about it…

You can easily be an influencer to a kid—read, interact, mentor, praise specifically, encourage, engage.

iPhony

The announcement that yet another Apple product is hitting the streets reminds me of Paul Revere letting everyone know, "The British are coming!" Everyone reacts and responds…well, at least those who have to have the latest, greatest gadget in their hands, or ears. It is amazing how technology, which used to be a nice convenience and a useful tool, has now become a vital appendage, as if the device were a human being. We respond to our devices, we act based on what they tell us, and some people will tell you that now they can't live without them.

What if we all got excited on a regular basis about things that really mattered in Hawai'i—like cleaning up beaches or painting schools or providing long-term answers for the homeless or resolving teacher contracts in a timely, professional manner? What if, instead of getting excited about a phone that's got more pixels, weighs a few ounces less, or provides a picture that's a tiny bit larger, we all got excited about things that have much greater impact to our communities and maybe even our own lives? I know this might not appeal to those younger viewers who drive the iRevolution, but maybe it's time to pass on the latest and greatest and look elsewhere for satisfaction.

What if everyone who stood in line—and will do so again in nine months, or six months, or one year—stood in line to feed the hungry or dropped food off at the food bank this weekend? What if some of the 10 million people who just have to have the new gizmo reflected on how to make a difference and tweeted their friends and got their Facebook pals to do something philanthropic? I bet that would feel better than yet another device that will become obsolete within a year. Feel better, do better, be better—now there's a revolutionary idea that doesn't involve 4G, maybe just gee whiz. Think about it…

I'd love to respond and even do something, but I'm too busy on my phone watching these really cute cats play piano.

Think about it.

Courage, Post-Crisis

Any sane person would agree that the issue of child sexual exploitation and underage prostitution need serious attention and action. And while everyone would agree with measures aimed at curbing this horrible practice, which exists here and elsewhere, too little attention is paid to what happens when victims are found, when runaways are rescued, when teenagers are brought in. Hawai'i's incarceration rate of juvenile girls exceeds the national average. Of these offenses, about 35 percent are runaways. Hawai'i has one of the highest rates of intrafamilial sexual abuse (or incest) and also has one of the highest attempted teen suicide rates in the nation. There are approximately 300 children reported missing in Hawai'i each month, many of them repeat runaways. There are no law enforcement statistics for child sex trafficking because of the lack of a state sex trafficking law.

Efforts have begun to develop a safe house, a solution for underage girls who may not be able to go back home given the depth of their trauma. Fundraising for this home here is underway, as a fledgling entity called Courage House is looking for land at an undisclosed O'ahu location to safely house and hopefully transform, educate, and rehabilitate these precious lives that have been sucked into the vicious cycle of sex trafficking and enslavement. Currently, there are Courage Houses in Sacramento and in the African nation of Tanzania. With over 100,000 estimated children and adolescents becoming involved in the US sex industry annually, we need to do more than simply promote awareness of this sordid situation. We need to help heal the wounded. We must rescue and restore.

Make no mistake about it, young victims fall prey to threats, Stockholm syndrome, and adult dependency, sometimes as an extension of abuses suffered at home. Rescuing these victims is one component, but giving them a chance to thrive for the next 70 years of their lives is something else. Want more information? Go to www.courageworldwide.org and see how you might make a difference in this ugly human tragedy. Think about it...

Think about it

October 25, 2012

Ballot Bailout

I have often lamented Hawai'i's woeful voting numbers, the apparent lack of interest—"ainokea" in local terms. I wondered if people really believed that their vote didn't matter, that our system was going to do what it would do no matter who got into local office. But at least it wasn't as bad as some other systems throughout the country, like Chicago or New Orleans where the joke was "Vote early and vote often." Or cities where deceased people voted. Or Washington, DC, where a crack user got reelected as mayor. Or the Deep South, where representatives who slept in congressional sessions in their 90s got reelected without a problem.

But maybe I was wrong. After years of witnessing voting machine problems and with the recent primary debacle on the Big Island, I wonder if maybe the apathetic were right, to some degree. For you see, "Vote early and vote often" is now alive and well in Mānoa, as duplicate ballots were mailed to over 800 voters in the area right above the University of Hawai'i. Those absentee voters are being told to destroy their ballots and wait for new ones, but if you mailed in the old ones already, then destroy the new ones when they arrive. Compounding things, voters received two blue envelopes with ballots, not just one. And the next ballot will be a single ballot, in a white envelope, of course. What's on first? No, who's on first? I don't know—third base!

The error was a machine duplicating error of course, as we live in an age and state where humans apparently are incapable of making mistakes and certainly are not accountable. Just ask UH. To err is no longer human, apparently. But please, do vote—just once, thank you—and let your voice be heard. And in Mānoa, just make sure it's just your singular voice and not a duet. Think about it…

Endorse-less

I find it disingenuous for news entities to tell you who to vote for. I think generally that news organizations should report the news, not be the news. Thus, you won't find me pontificating tonight about why this candidate is better than that one. By now, hopefully, you have glossed over enough information to make your own decisions. After all, you're at least 18 years old and decision-making is something you should be accustomed to, on your own.

There's something hypocritical when news organizations take on the air of neutrality in reporting the news when an in-house editorial board tells us who it thinks we should vote for. A factual explanation of what each candidate stands for is a better way of presenting information to the soon-to-be-voting public than a ringing endorsement in print or over the air. After all, if I continue to follow your news organization, can I safely assume that your reporting will be based on facts, and not your resentment or happiness over who lost or who won?

If most issues have two points of view, can I be sure to get a fair assessment of issues when you've already told me which side you favor? It's sad that too often nowadays various news media are perceived to blatantly swing one way or the other. When I want slanted opinions, I just ask a relative or a neighbor; I get what I expect. But under the banner of journalism and fact and information sharing, too many media blowhards aim to shock or share simply to draw a larger audience than the competition. It's pandering and showcases their insincere front as a supposed news organization. Gathering opinions is one thing. Sharing in-house opinions and calling it news is false advertising.

A recent joint MIT/Stanford study of the effect of newspaper and electronic media endorsements found that the potential voter was more likely to be impacted by a media endorsement based on his or her own feeling of the media source's ideological bent—did it tend to be perceived as leaning left or right. Endorsements are often information shortcuts for some people, and that's a shame. Bottom line—make up your own mind, get the facts by Tuesday, and then make your decision based on what you think is best for you and us. And then vote. Think about it…

"'Twas the Night" Revisited

'Twas the weekend before Christmas, and all through the house
Not a creature was stirring, except for the clicking of that incessant
    computer mouse.
The stockings were hung by the chimney with care;
Heck, they cost ten bucks each, so I used them to wear.
The children were nestled all snug in their beds,
While visions from Facebook danced in their heads.
And Mamma in her muʻumuʻu and I in my cap,
Had just settled down from shopping at The Gap.
When out on the lawn there arose such a clatter,
I sprang up from bed, though I've grown a bit fatter.
Away to the window I flew like a flash,
Propped open old louvers, but a faulty one crashed.
When, what to my wandering eyes should appear,
A guy rummaging for cans, and I just sighed, "Oh dear."
Now darn it, now come on, now this can't be so,
In a land of such plenty, yet some have no dough.
His eyes—how they twinkled! His dimples, how merry!
His demeanor so pleasant; his fragrant lei plumeri(a).
He spoke not a word but kept straight at his work,
I said nary a word lest he think me a jerk.
As he turned to continue his trek in the night,
He looked at me, smiled, and said, "It's all right."
And I realize this season brings happiness and joy,
But let's help each other, with goodness deployed.
Merry Christmas, Hawaiʻi, and to all a good night!
Continue the fine fight to always do right;
We must do what we can, we must never ever quit,
We must always be conscious, and think about it…

Think about it ⸝ₗₗ꜀

January 17, 2013

Warriors as Winners

The Wounded Warrior Amputee Softball Team did its thing here last week, proving that even with disabilities, these veterans remain undaunted. The athletic skill and positive attitudes displayed by this traveling athletic squad of America's best warmed the hearts of parents and kids at hospitals and tested Hawai'i's able-bodied military softballers and a bunch of media celebrities on softball battle fields throughout the week.

The premise for these prosthetic pros doing their thing is most inspiring—showing people of all stripes that no matter what life throws at you or takes from you, you can still put your best out there and thrive, not merely survive. We live in an age where people share their thoughts like germs, letting friends and even disinterested networking zombies know about their bad hair days, what they put on their hot dog at lunch, and how upset they were about not getting a better parking space at the mall.

These brave dingers of the diamond faced death while serving our nation and still face uncertainty and challenges while sharing their gifts of softball excellence and life lessons. Live life it to its fullest, because you never know what's around the bend. That's not paranoia, just reality, and seeing this team do its thing is believing. Motivation here comes from role models who have persevered through adversity and can be an inspiration to all of us if we'll simply put down our cell phones, stop whining, and focus more often on all that we've got. Lesson learned. These wandering warriors may be wounded, but their healthy spirits lift the soul. They may not win all of their games, but they are undoubtedly champions. Think about it.

Think about it.

Lessons Learned?

A couple of lessons have been learned, sadly, over the past month or so: Lesson #1: When something seems too good to be true, it often is. Whether it's a sales deal that requires you to read the fine print, a web or direct marketing come-on, or an avatar girlfriend that you apparently connect with solely through cyberspace and cell phone calls, be skeptical. There are bad and devious people out there, just looking to make a buck or enhance their own sorry lives, so do your homework, ask questions, and maintain your sanity.

Lesson #2: We have apparently become rather desensitized to violence in this country. When 12 high school students and a teacher were killed in 1999 at Colorado's Columbine High School, that was tragic. When 29 college and graduate students and three professors were gunned down at Virginia Tech in 2007, that was horrible. But apparently it took the stunning murder of 20 little children and six adults in a Connecticut elementary school last month to get people to say we need to discuss guns in America. Really? Were we numb, scared, or blind to the need for at least a serious discussion after the incidents in Colorado or Virginia, or after the movie theater massacre in Aurora, Colorado? Better mental health services and training? Armed guards at every school? Who's going to pay for that when social services and police forces continue to get chopped by cash-strapped municipalities?

We have the right to free speech in this country (that right is chronologically listed before the right to bear arms), but you can't yell "Fire!" in a crowded theater or use dirty language on broadcast TV. We earn a license to drive a car, but you can't go 90 miles per hour. Can we really have a civil discussion and look at reality in 2013 as it relates to freedom on the internet and its costs and the relative freedom of gun ownership? Or do we want to just accept that that's the way things go sometimes in a democracy; ho hum, pass the chips and dip. Think about it…

Enough with the shallow, redundant, unhelpful post-trauma "thoughts and prayers" routine. While the United States is home to just over four percent of the world's population, it's estimated to be the home of more than 40 percent of the total guns available in the world.

Think about it.

February 11, 2013

Larry

How well do you know the person in the cubicle next to you at work, the one who takes care of your stuff when you're out sick or on vacation? How well do you know the neighbor next door who takes in your mail when you're out of town or picks up your garbage can when it's knocked over? Now you might say you know them as well as you want to, but maybe if you knew a bit more, you would be greatly enriched and enlightened, like I was with Larry.

I worked with Larry for over 20 years; said hi, exchanged pleasantries, but never went much deeper than that because I didn't have to, because I was too busy, because he tended to be a bit shy, and maybe because I was the boss and didn't want to pry. Yet it took a eulogy at Larry's funeral last month for me to find out some amazing things—like the fact that Larry loved to play the 'ukulele, that Larry at one time thought of being a priest. Or that Larry was a radio operator during the Vietnam War whose life was saved by a heroic colleague who jumped on a live enemy grenade, thus sacrificing his life for Larry and the others. Apparently, Larry wondered for 40 years why he survived and his friend didn't that day. A moment like that changes you forever; it changed Larry, no doubt. I gained a new appreciation for Larry; for his humble demeanor; his amazing, dual 40-hour-a-week jobs; and his pleasant demeanor while he just got the job done, day after day, year after year, always wondering.

What I learned in the succinct stories at Larry's funeral and what I realize more often now as I get older is that people have depth, everybody has wondrous stories, and while we're all busy, distracted, and sometimes disinterested, there's a lot of good stuff going on out there if we just try to find it…in everybody. Think about it…

Think about it..

Government Defined

New Zealand's Local Government Act of 2002 states that the purpose of local government is to enable democratic local decision-making and action by, and on behalf of, communities; and to promote the social, economic, environmental, and cultural well-being of communities, in the present and for the future. Sounds reasonable to me, but the devil is always in the details and in the eye of the beholder.

Recently, local government here has made overtures to tax soft drinks, mandate larger fines on negligent property owners, clean sidewalks of tents and other items, and has recommended many other so-called fixes to our society as always occurs during the short legislative session. So when does government overstep its boundaries? When does it go too far? When does it impede too far Into the lives of the very citizens it is supposed to be helping but not manhandling? Well, that answer usually depends on your perspective and your personal situation.

Too much government? Perhaps not when it comes to repairing our roads and upgrading our public schools; not when it comes to protecting our country, our wildlife, and our shorelines; not when it comes to my earned Social Security, Medicare, and Medicaid checks. Disgruntled people say they want government to stay out of their lives, and rightfully so in some cases, but they sure like knowing that local authorities are working on solving crime problems in their neighborhoods. It's a battle of balancing our needs and our rights while not overstepping the granted power of authority. So right now, you need to speak up at the local legislative level to help ensure that your voice is heard and, most importantly, listened to. That's part of government's role, too. Think about it...

Concert Connection

Country star Alan Jackson just held a successful concert at the Blaisdell Arena on Sunday night, and the inimitable Carlos Santana is in town for shows this week on Oʻahu and on Maui. It's great when top national and international acts bring their songs to Hawaiʻi; we just need to see more of them. Local sensation Bruno Mars recently announced a domestic concert tour, and at the present time, Hawaiʻi is not on the list of his summertime stops.

The reason as to why major artists don't often perform in Hawaiʻi as often as they used to has to do primarily with money—the cost of shipping stage sets and props, the cost of flying out a large entourage, the cost of the downtime between Hawaiʻi and the next stop on the tour. It's much easier to travel cross-country with vans than it is to load up a plane or two for a special show here. Plus, we have venue limitations, with nothing available on Oʻahu between the 8,700-seat Blaisdell Arena and the 50,000-seat Aloha Stadium. While many top acts can command a crowd of 15,000 or 20,000, that number of tickets would require two nights (and more cost) at the Blaisdell or Stand Sheriff Center and for the biggest acts, 15,000 or even 20,000 fans at Aloha Stadium simply wouldn't cover all of the associated concert costs.

So while we happily accept the artists and promoters that still find a way to make it work here, we also pine for the good old days when top acts would play three or four nights of sold-out shows on Oʻahu or fill Aloha Stadium when multiple acts performed for hours during a weekend afternoon and evening. We may be in a new era of mobile dexterity, but watching someone's YouTube cell phone camera shots of mainland concerts just doesn't provide the same buzz of witnessing a live show in paradise. Think about it...

Bruno Mars (three times), The Eagles, Guns N' Roses, Snoop Dogg, Eminem—all in a recent six-month window at Aloha Stadium? Miracles do happen! Stay tuned.

Happy Hawai'i

A recent Gallup well-being poll shows Hawai'i to be the top state in the nation for the fourth consecutive year. People here are apparently pretty satisfied with their lives, their physical and emotional health, and even liked the places they work in. The ranking is based on year-round surveying of 353,000 respondents throughout the country, with about a thousand people here included in the annual tally.

While the results may not be a surprise to those of us who live here and find ourselves smiling more often than many of our mainland compatriots, it was interesting to note that other states at the top of the happy and healthy list include Colorado, Minnesota, Utah, Vermont, Montana, Nebraska, and New Hampshire. So there is certainly no warm-weather geographical skew to this survey, as balmy days or access to an ocean are obviously not criteria for how people feel and think about their daily plight in life or their sense of personal satisfaction.

As a matter of fact, looking at the states listed right below us, you might think that a predominance of cold weather, snow, and hours spent indoors are facets that make people happy; but perhaps they just work and live around those subjective discomforts in these content states. Nonetheless, it's nice to be number one, it's nice to be here, and it's nice to be nice and happy, which Hawai'i people are as a rule, also confirmed via tweets that were aggregated for this study, too. But we knew that anyway, didn't we? Think about it…

Public protests on various fronts throughout the Islands indicate that happiness is relative and not guaranteed. Decision makers had better prepare to explain themselves and their plans in more detail and more often, or face passionate resistance.

Think about it.

March 18, 2013

They're Baaack!

They're coming from everywhere, and that's good news. More visitors from more places means the tourism industry is literally spreading the wealth, which bodes well if one area suddenly contracts or if the airline lift—or total number of seats coming and going—drops off. They're coming from Taiwan and South Korea as well as from Japan, from New Zealand, as well as from Australia. The East Coast business from the mainland is strong, and those visitors actually spend more than West Coast travelers here.

And with more seats and markets come more opportunities for the valued business travelers, along with more meetings and conventions here. With retrofits at many Waikīkī and Neighbor Island properties in recent years, the guest experience at hotels should be better than ever. And a vibrant tourist economy is obviously the biggest indicator of a strong local economy in the months and years ahead.

When times are tough, some argue we need to diversify our tourism industry—give 'em new reasons to come here. When times are good, everyone relaxes a bit and smiles. But we really do need more plans for recreation, ecotourism, and new activities, while making sure that the infrastructures are sound on our roads, at our parks and beaches, and in our hotels. When it comes to tourism, looks like the surf's up, and the waves of visitors should be rolling in for the foreseeable future. Think about it…

Well, we were happy up to a degree with the return of visitors when the recession ended—but for many locals, not so much now.

March 25, 2013

To Pay or Not To Pay

Money and quality—sometimes you can't get one without the other. Sometimes you can. Over and over again, the past few weeks we have seen contentious issues arise regarding pay raises or salaries for librarians and top local officials. People who don't know the details about what it takes to find the best people for high-profile positions and then pay them accordingly, reflexively say we can't afford high salaries for these positions in times of austerity.

But reality and history tell us that it's often hard to find top people for top jobs in Hawai'i, and saving some money to hire perceptibly lower-quality candidates who will work for less can certainly cost you more in the long run. If comparable pay vis-à-vis other markets for similar positions is the baseline for how we pay certain people in Hawai'i, then there really shouldn't be much arguing over what's fair. Legislators met last month with UH brass to assess salaries at UH. If legislators truly want a relatively autonomous university that attracts the best and the brightest—at all levels—it might have to back off and accept the current state of what it takes monetarily to attract those assumed top people.

And that reality needs to be realized not just when it comes to salaries at the university level—it also goes for many other state and city positions. We can save some here and there, and we should always negotiate a "fair" salary, but generically suggesting that librarians, university hierarchy, and other highly paid officials are overpaid could result in a short-term savings with long-term losses when the wrong person is hired to save a few bucks today. Think about it…

Micromanagement of UH still reigns supreme when the legislature rolls up its sleeves and looks for someone or something to blame for annual financial shortfalls.

Think about it

March 28, 2013

UH Athletics and Reality

The University of Hawaiʻi Mānoa on behalf of its athletics department is apparently going to ask the UH Board of Regents to forgive its ever-growing athletics department debt, which will reach upwards of $13 million by the end of this fiscal year on June 30. Whether or not it's forgiven, something needs to be done to rectify the inequities of this Division I program. The UH athletics department has been asked to run itself more like a business, but is that realistic in today's challenging college landscape when the athletics department has its hands tied behind its back like few other comparable institutions.

UH pays rent to play football, it doesn't get a fair share of concessions from the Rainbowtique, it doesn't share in parking revenue when you come on campus to park specifically for an athletic event, and it gets less in state funding than any other state schools it competes against. So asking UH sports to fix its financial woes in the face of these realities is a bit like asking a guy in a leaky boat to keep rowing to shore, without plugging or even acknowledging the obvious holes…

One possible way to reassess things would be to simply plan for and accept an annual deficit of $2 to $3 million, which would still be a smaller loss than realized by most institutions in the so-called Football Bowl Subdivision. Yes, despite raking in billions of dollars in television, ticket, and licensing revenues, all but 14 of the 106 schools in the NCAA's top athletic division lost money in 2009. Only 17 of 300 Division I athletic programs made money between 2004 and 2006. Only 10 percent of 227 Division I public school athletic programs made money in 2011. The median loss for all schools was over $10 million. So let's give UH a fair chance and either provide more state subsidies, unpleasant as it may sound, allow revenue to funnel to athletics when it's due to athletics, or get realistic about expectations to turn a so-called profit year after year. Think about it…

The role of annually beleaguered UH athletics director David Matlin will be played by quirky Bill Murray in this version of Groundhog Day 2.

April 22, 2013

Context in a Nonstop World

Too many events last week were stunning or even numbing in nature. The tragedy at the Boston Marathon; the tragedy of a huge explosion in West, Texas; and finally, for me, the tragic loss locally of a 15-year-old in a skateboarding accident. With the advent of 24-hour news, 24-hour sports, cell phone pictures, texting, instant maps, and social media, it seems that not a day or an hour goes by where we're not told something that is supposed to make us sit up and take notice, or at least pay attention. If you miss an hour, you're considered uninformed.

Bad things happen to good people, this is a sad fact of life. Bad people do bad things in life, such is the nature of man's innate free will. I just wonder sometimes if we all might be better off to ponder some of what's going on in silence, without updates, without constant reminders, without bombardment from everyone and everything around us. It's hard to put jarring things in perspective when the next thing comes at us within 15 minutes. Maybe we could come to grips easier with some traumas if we just had some time to breathe, to reflect, and then to move on.

But that won't just happen anymore. You're going to have to actively find a quiet corner or park or sanctuary to collect your thoughts or spend time with a loved one and come to grips with what's going on. Our apparently never-ending thirst to be told, informed, and updated has surely desensitized us to some degree. Amateurs overanalyze from across the street or even across the airwaves, but at the end of the day, which nowadays never seems to end with electronic information availability 24/7, we're still frail humans trying to gain context when perhaps it can best come from within, if we just give it some time. Think about it…

April 29, 2013

The Business of Travel

One of the areas that is feeding the growth in our local tourism industry is business travel. More meeting and convention planners are deciding that Hawai'i really is a fine place to hold a gathering, either for rewards or as incentives, or even as a site to hold an annual meeting or convention for a large group. It wasn't that long ago that we all heard the age-old story about how businesses simply couldn't justify excursions to Hawai'i, as it was perceived that our paradise was a boondoggle or an unnecessary expense.

But that was before the economic picture brightened and perhaps before some people did their homework and realized that we do have fine convention facilities, up-to-date technical capabilities, and a decent infrastructure that enables hotels throughout O'ahu and on the Neighbor Islands to deal with large crowds. Some of those wrong assumptions about the quality of business travel facilities in Hawai'i were made before a very successful APEC conference here proved that Hawai'i can hold its own with many so-called business meeting destinations.

While business travelers convened with no second thoughts for years in markets like New York, Las Vegas, or San Francisco, some saw Hawai'i as simply too far away, too extravagant, or incapable of meeting needs for meetings. But nothing breeds success like positive experiences and solid word of mouth. The future continues to brighten for even more large business gatherings in our islands, and that will provide a nice boost to our major economic driver—tourism. Business travelers book well in advance, are very organized, and pay incrementally higher room rates than leisure travelers. It's a win-win scenario for local business and excited, satisfied visitors. Now if we can just make it easier for local businesses to do business here… Think about it…

Far too often, we still can't break through the perception that Hawai'i is not a viable business meeting location, and it's not only about the cost.

May 6, 2013

Natation at the Natatorium

Finally. Well, maybe. It appears that we have absolute local leadership consensus on what to do with the dilapidated natatorium at the end of Waikīkī Beach. After years of neglect, slow deterioration, politics, myriad suggestions, and failed fundraising efforts, the natatorium will apparently be torn down to make way for a public beach, with the 86-year-old facility's archway getting a much-needed restoration and moving about 50 feet away from the beach.

Some opposed to tearing down the bleachers and such will say this is heresy and a slap in the face based on the original intent of this World War I memorial, but letting rusty metal bars and crumbling stones—unsafe for human usage—sit and deteriorate year after year while one administration after another unveils promises annually unfulfilled is a complete waste of time and is also a slight on the memory of those honored by the natatorium's existence.

Ah, but now the fun begins—who will pay for the repair work, the city or the state? Hopefully, the money matters can be quickly resolved and work can begin in short order, but if history is to be our guide, don't bet on it. After all, the swimming pool there has been closed for 34 years, a testament to government indecision and the city council and state legislature have other major funding issues and priorities to deal with, as always. So while this supposedly definitive announcement is a relief and long overdue, don't plan that beach party or baby lū'au just yet at the renovated Kaimana Beach landmark. Think about it...

Nothing, nada, nil, zippo, zero, zilch—except more studies and promises. Maybe when a visiting 12-year-old from Nashville gets skewered on exposed Natatorium rebar someone will act.

Think about it

May 23, 2013

Musical Notes

We need a big-time music festival in Hawai'i. Maybe something could be worked up for the spring or fall during a lull in the tourist season, and at a time when other annual festivals are not going on. We need a fenced-off park on O'ahu or a Neighbor Island with craft booths, food, festivities, and great live music including local and top domestic and international talent. I mean, if people are willing to go to Manchester, Tennessee, for Bonnaroo; and Indio, California, for Coachella, why can't we put on a world-class event in Hawai'i? Make it a three-day affair to encourage people to spend a week in Hawai'i.

We also need to revisit holding concert events at the Stan Sheriff Center. It's a great venue; centrally located and sits relatively idle for four months each year between May and August. Yeh, I know the Stevie Wonder thing didn't work out, but having concerts at UH that somehow benefit UH and include discounts for UH students would provide an opportunity to gain value from a wonderful, but underutilized, facility.

And what ever happened to Andrews Amphitheatre? It used to be a great summertime concert venue for mainland and local acts—Blue Oyster Cult, The Animals, Peter Moon's Kanikapila, Shaggy, Bob Dylan, Bruddah Iz, The Green—many great artists over many years, under the stars, but it's used far too infrequently of late. In summary, I am pushing for more music of all sorts locally, for music is the universal language that really does bring people together. Enjoy the Hoku Awards on KFVE on Saturday night, celebrating the best Hawai'i has to offer these days in the world of music. Tap your toes, hum along, and think about it…

May 27, 2013

Skyline Redo

Every time you look up these days, someone is making plans for a new high-rise in the Kakaʻako corridor. From mixed-purpose buildings to condos to a Cineplex and a new concert facility, plans are grand at this stage. And with those plans come many questions. And what of the effects on infrastructure, parking, density, traffic, and the commercial/residential mix? All questions that need to be thoroughly vetted and worked out for these projects to come to fruition and provide a quality experience for residents, shoppers, and passersby.

One of the big questions is just that—how big is too big? A height variance to allow buildings to go up to 700 feet is being proposed. Our downtown looks stunted to some, based on the old rules about height limits. Might Kakaʻako become the beacon in the sky as the area with the tallest buildings in Hawaiʻi? Could be if the variances allowing for building height changes are approved. By the time the work is done—if everything comes to fruition—it would mean about two dozen new buildings in the Kakaʻako area would have been built over a period of about 30 years.

As the population base on Oʻahu has spread westward and eastward over the past 30 years, apparently real estate entrepreneurs see now as the time to not only grow in the core of Honolulu, but also to grow up Honolulu by constructing buildings almost double the size of most our existing tall buildings. The citizens, legal eagles, and environmentalists will have their say, and then the business interests will really decide if all of these announced projects make sense. But big change is a-coming to Kakaʻako over the next decade or so, that much is for sure. Think about it…

Big changes have come to Kakaʻako; now we just need to create more legitimately affordable units somewhere for younger folks trying to stay here and make ends meet. Perhaps incentivizing builders would help move things along, because from a business standpoint, why would a builder build $400,000 units when he can quickly sell million-dollar units? And local homeowners want their home values to go up. Supply and demand are not making it easier for first-time buyers in Hawai`i.

Think about it.

June 20, 2013

Spiraling Stairway

It's only been about 26 years of waiting, so let's hope that the Honolulu City Council can render some opinion and final decisions on the Ha'ikū Stairs soon. Or the council could wait another 26 years, thus matching the time frame on a decision on the Waikīkī natatorium issue, and the so-called Stairway to Heaven will simply continue to deteriorate and maybe fall apart, which might really limit access. Case closed!

Last week, visitors got lost looking for the 70-year-old stairs. Others have been known to sneak up there before sunrise and before the guard comes on duty to politely tell people to go away, that the stairs are not open to the public. One website blogger bragged about sneaking past a sleeping guard. The city pays over $50,000 per year for the security detail. Local Kāne'ohe residents don't like the intrusion in their neighborhood and yards. People get cited for trespassing, people get lost, and yet the stairs are still there, somewhat guarded, and people are still willing to take on a security officer, darkness, possibly surly neighbors, and Mother Nature for the chance to witness the panoramic views from on high.

At a late March meeting of the Honolulu City Council's Parks Committee, it was decided that various council representatives would take a hike to the trail, to help them render an opinion. Why it took until 2013 for that idea to arise is stunning. It's now late-June, and nothing more has been done, but it's been that way for years, and this scenario is symptomatic of far too many local issues that get pushed aside rather than dealt with for fear of angering some constituent base. People are elected to make decisions, not avoid them. In the classic song, "Stairway To Heaven," Led Zeppelin told us not to be alarmed "…if there's a bustle in your hedgerow." Well, before someone falls, dies, or gets attacked in the wee a.m. hours, let's react to this bustle in our hedgerow now and figure out what to do about our very real Stairway to Heaven. Think about it…

For reference, see Waikīkī Natatorium editorials—aka zilch, nada, nothing. Blustery bureaucratic babbling, benign bumbling, and bewildering bantering.

Fruits of Our Desire

I was driving up a street that had a bit of an uphill incline the other day and there were no other cars or people around. Suddenly, I noticed a lone mango rolling down the street by the curb. I thought, how unique, to see a piece of live fruit rolling along, like it was on its way to the store or a movie. And then I started to think about how lucky we are to have items like mangos, papayas, lychees, guavas, liliko'i, and other succulent products that we enjoy year-round in Hawai'i.

Now, pondering our local fruit options might not seem like a worthwhile endeavor, but it sure beats texting and driving, and I did keep my focus on the road while my thoughts drifted to a quiet morning with an indulgence of chilled papaya and a splash of lime. I actually prefer papaya to mango. And I realized that while I love vacationing on Neighbor Islands and enjoying the hotel service provided along the way, I really should start more of my work mornings by savoring a local fruit of choice rather than rushing out the door with a sugar-drenched yogurt cup or store-bought smoothie in a bottle.

Now I know this may not be my heaviest topic of the year, but having these delectable tropical treats so readily available is just one more reason you can say, "Lucky you live Hawai'i." And as for the mango meandering its way down the street when I drove by the other day, maybe he or she was just out for a walk. By the way, know how you make a mango shake? Take it to a scary movie. Think about it…

August 26, 2013

Mighty Murph

When someone's job description lends itself to acts of bravery and courage, it's hard for these people to see themselves as heroes. Just ask any military war veteran, police officer, or firefighter. "I was just doing my job" is the likely refrain when asked about acts of bravery and putting them self in harm's way. Now Antoinette Tuff, a school bookkeeper who talked a hostage taker in an Atlanta-area school into putting his weapons down—she's a hero.

So how do you define heroism or heroic deeds? Well, I would like to offer for your consideration under the term "hero" one Don Murphy. Yeh, it's a different kind of hero, but here's a guy who, alongside his incredible and equally hardworking wife Marion, runs a single Irish bar and restaurant in downtown Honolulu. Yet year after year, event after event, good ole Murph is out there working his tail off, organizing, cooking, serving, and donating food and time. You want to talk about the aloha spirit? Don Murphy could be a poster child. Whether it's his recent Pigskin Pigout for the UH football team, his efforts serving sliders at the Sony Open or other golf events, his meals donated to the Sheraton Hawaii Bowl, his Merchant Street outdoor fundraisers for children's cancer research, the list goes on and on, year after year.

He is a booster of local life, not just local sports. He is a living treasure, a bona fide hero who people count on to help them meet their financial goals and/or to help them provide a quality event. So next time you're thinking about where to grab a bite downtown, show some love to a guy who radiates aloha and humbly does his thing for all of us time after time. Visit Murphy's Bar & Grill, where the food is great and the employees are wonderful, and go see a real-life, living local legend. Take your kids; show 'em what a hero looks like. Think about it…

Murph and Marion continue to do their thing here for so many so often.

Think about it

August 29, 2013

Work: The Pits or the Passion

At a recent luncheon here, I listened to renown speaker/psychologist Bruce Christopher tell the tale of a longtime study done with thousands of people who were asked about their number one priority in a job search. 83 percent said money, 17 percent said finding a job that they could be passionate about. Fast-forward 20 years, and the group was interviewed again. 101 people from this group of thousands had become millionaires. One person out of that 101 came from the "money first" priority list, while 100 people who had made their fortune came from the passion side of the ledger.

The moral might be find what you love, or find something to love, and then pursue it, passionately. Much like a personal relationship, just showing up every day doesn't make for great fulfillment. But if you can find something that you really enjoy during most of your working hours, you will be deeply enriched, even if you never get close to becoming a millionaire. Yes, we can't always be at the perfect job, but our happiness, sense of value and self-worth, and our attitudes most surely affect all of the other areas of our lives, so why not try to work at something that potentially fulfills you, much like a personal relationship should help you to feel whole.

It's a tough job market out there in Hawai'i for both rookies and veterans, but if you strive to find a workplace or career path that provides you with those things that matter most to you, it sure can help to make even the toughest days of work that much more worthwhile. We should encourage young people to go for it—to reach out and find their place. Simply showing up every day is not only mundane, but also stifling. As life is most assuredly a journey and not a destination, make sure you check out the sights along the way in your quest for happiness and fulfillment at work. Think about it…

Think about it..

September 16, 2013

North Shore Shirking

If a meeting was held and no one showed up, would it still be a meeting? Well, a meeting was held a week ago in a crowded North Shore school cafeteria and a lot of people showed up. So, yes, it was a meeting. But no one showed up from the state Department of Transportation, the people who control the road fronting Laniākea Beach and who could really make a difference for frustrated local residents. The traffic situation has been awful on the North Shore for years when surf events take place or when sea turtle sightings drive hundreds or thousands of people out to this beautiful area—both locals and tourists, spectators, turtle fans, and surfers.

While discussions have been ongoing for years and while everyone has expressed frustration over people parking poorly and darting across the street precariously, there is still no solution in sight. The local area state representative and other officials assured the crowd that their voices were being heard, but people want to know when definitive action will be taken. The DOT says it will meet on the issue soon. While barricades go up in certain areas, some in the agitated crowd wondered why there seems to be no urgency to develop a long-term plan to restrict access or provide peace of mind and safety in the neighborhood.

The state has concerns about liability issues if it takes action, but who will be liable right now if an accident takes a life? Shirking responsibility on the single artery and on the beaches is not an answer. A beach park adjacent to Laniākea Beach was proposed…two decades ago. Sea turtles can live for well over a hundred years, and a real solution for North Shore traffic reduction and safer access points for interested turtle and surf gawkers might take that long to appear. Ducking one's head into one's shell is not what officials were elected for, no matter how tough a situation appears to be. Think about it…

See also the Waikīkī Natatorium, the Falls of Clyde, Ha'iku Stairway to Heaven… and the list goes on.

October 7, 2013

Smoke Screened

The University of Hawaiʻi Mānoa will strengthen its policy against smoking on January 1 when it bans the use of all tobacco products and electronic cigarettes anywhere on campus and within 50 feet of the campus. Good for UH. The decision points out the hypocrisy in this country whereby we allow cigarettes, a proven killer, to be readily available, yet we continue to demonize all forms of recreational drugs, some of which are surely less dangerous or addictive than nicotine. The point here is not to question whether or not to legalize certain recreational drugs—that's a different discussion—but rather to ask: Why are cigarettes still legal in this country?

400,000 die annually in the United States due to cigarette smoking, and tens of thousands are adversely affected by secondhand smoke. Healthcare costs in the US related to smoking are $100 billion a year. Nicotine is highly addictive; many Americans try to kick the habit each year, but the National Institute of Health says that 85 percent of those who try to quit on their own relapse within one week! Drug levels from smoke inhalation peak within 10 seconds—now that's a quick high. So aside from the economic value to a few states and the amazing power of the tobacco lobby in Washington, DC, you have to ask yourself: Why isn't this drug illegal?

If you think you aren't affected as a nonsmoker, think again. Nicotine and smoking sicken even nonsmokers, and everyone's insurance rates are affected over time to help cover the ailments. Smoking decreases one's life expectancy by 8.3 years, or about 12 minutes per cigarette. Tobacco kills more people in this country annually than AIDS, alcohol, car accidents, illegal drugs, murders, and suicides…combined. It is long overdue for the US to ban this wicked and addictive product in all forms, as politically treacherous as it might seem. And for the 19 percent of Americans who still smoke, a ban will ultimately be an obvious blessing. Think about it…

In 2019, there were more than 480,000 deaths in the US attributed to smoking, including 10 percent related to secondhand smoke. And now vaping is an issue?

DC Auwē

You might have missed it with all of the mass confusion, posturing, and bantering in Washington, DC, over the past few weeks, but here's something that just might not surprise you. What do potholes, hemorrhoids, and dog poop have in common? Well, according to a recent poll done by Public Policy Polling, these items are all more popular than Congress. And lest you think that this unpopularity is a new phenomenon brought on by the government shutdown, Congress's current eight percent approval rating is not far off of the 10 percent approval rating from last year. Ebola, heroin, Honey Boo Boo, and Vladmir Putin do rank lower on the popularity scale, thank goodness.

People in the poll said they had a higher opinion of cockroaches and toenail fungus than they do of our elected Washington, DC, officials. But perhaps what's saddest about the debacle that is Washington, DC, these days is that the people who have made this mess seem not to care. They remain oblivious to what real people think or go through—yes, the very people who elect them in the first place. To prove a point, to cater to special interest groups and powerful lobbying entities, our democratically elected officials have sold their souls and, perhaps, their brains.

Power and control, that's what one DC lobbyist told me is all that really matters and is fought for in the halls of our Congress—and that sentiment was shared with me 25 years ago. The rancor and discordant tone that comes from decisions and lack thereof in our nation's capital is embarrassing and ongoing, and it affects real people right here in Hawai'i and elsewhere every single day. Alas, there may not be a better system by which to govern, but the people in charge really do need to set their egos and career aspirations aside to do what they were elected to do, or else…we'll just reelect them again. Hmmm. Think about it…

Nice to see that at least Putin has made a comeback in some people's eyes.

A&B See

There is an old sentiment or saying that "change is good." In reality, change is good, as long as it's good change. Kailua residents will find out soon enough just how good change is when Alexander & Baldwin takes over the real estate holdings of Kaneohe Ranch and the Harold K. L. Castle Foundation in a deal valued at $373 million. One thing for sure, no one pays $373 million and keeps things status quo. Rents will go up, the tenant mix will most assuredly change over time, and the very face of Kailua town will morph in the decades ahead.

Kailua is already mired in a battle to "Keep Kailua, Kailua," as the bumper stickers say. From efforts to reigning in the illegal bed and breakfast establishments to traffic concerns surrounding a new Target store at the old Don Quijote site to a shutdown of beach commerce, Kailua residents are never shy about letting their opinions be known about just how they want their slice of the island to be treated. A&B says it will include the community in development discussions, as it wants to be a good landowner. That's a good start, as the delicate balance between a suburban, friendly windward beach environment and a bustling shopping mecca for locals and tourists alike will require some heavy discourse as building and renovation projects invariably evolve over time.

What some will call progress, others will most assuredly call an abomination, an affront, an assault on the pastoral past of this vibrant community. But one thing is for certain in the investment world—no one these days pays $373 million and simply adds a few poinsettia planters and roundabouts. Think about it…

Kailua is no longer quaint with undiscovered nooks. It is often overrun with short-term renters, cyclists looking everywhere but at the traffic, and web-savvy travelers finding every heretofore hidden trail—then using your garden hose to clean off.

Think about it.

ʻAumakua Aloha

A few years back, I had a nasty health scare. While things are fine now, there was a great uncertainty when I heard the word from my doctor over the phone. I was alone and scared on the Big Island, without family and unwilling to talk about my situation as I awaited the start of KFVE's coverage of the Merrie Monarch Festival, and I was in stunned disbelief. I never got sick, never missed work, never had health issues; I was unbeatable and undefeated. Upon learning of my possible fate, I needed to do something, go somewhere to feel better, to get a sign that maybe, just maybe, things would be OK. I was in a daze.

I went to the Panaʻewa Rainforest Zoo to see Namaste, the white tiger. I always go there when in Hilo. I love tigers. Independent, graceful, and truly the underrated king of the jungle, as a tiger would most surely win a battle over a lion. Check out the research. I like the tiger's underdog status, its fight to survive extinction, and I love the colors. As a kid, I wanted to go to college at Princeton University, mostly because they are known as the Tigers. Anyway, I was in a real funk and was pretty much alone in the expansive park when I got to Namaste's tiger enclosure. I stood up top while Namaste basked in the sun at the bottom, about 75 yards away. I sighed, feeling even more alone and frightened, when suddenly, as if on cue, Namaste rose up and slowly made his way up the hill. He stopped right in front of me, quietly gazing at me and somehow peacefully assuring me that everything would be OK, just have faith. Well, at least that's how I saw it from my newfound ʻaumakua.

It is now 33 months later, and I am fine. But, alas, Namaste, who had an injured leg and a hip that degenerated over the years, was sadly, but mercifully, put to sleep recently at the age of 15, having outlived his siblings. Namaste is not gone. I have him deep in my soul, along with a stuffed animal replica in my office, and he will always be with me, just as he was when I most needed him that quiet, spring day, when I felt so helpless, vulnerable, and defeated. We all need a Namaste by our side, human or otherwise. Aloha, my friend. Think about it...

Today, eight years later, my health remains fine, and the tiger remains my beacon of strength, grace, beauty, confidence, and individuality.

Everything's Al-right

Media people by their very nature can often be skeptics, even cynics. Sometimes, they are really not those shiny, happy people you see on TV, listen to on the radio, or read in the daily paper. And then there was Al Chase. Al passed away last Thursday, and he was a difference maker. His early work on the soccer fields of Hawai'i helped pave the way for youths and adults alike in growing the game locally at Kalani High and elsewhere.

His dispassionate but objective coverage of Team Hawaii of the North American Soccer League in 1977 belied his true love for the game. For Al could be passionate, yet objective, a difficult chore when tasked with covering a sports franchise that was like the Titanic—full of possibilities but doomed to fail. He carried his zeal into his work covering our semi-pro soccer efforts in 1978 and 1979 for the Honolulu Star-Bulletin. His knowledge was deep, but he was always humble in my conversations with him. He gnashed his teeth at the pro team's mismanagement and ultimate departure for Tulsa, but he replied fairly.

I heard Al could be tough as nails as a coach, but when I learned the ropes from him at age 21, he was always fair, honest, and accurate. He was interesting and interested, a rare pair of platitudes too seldom found in a world where people need to always get in the last word or make the story about themselves. He was a closet cheerleader who loved all forms of local soccer and baseball, but always respected the distance he had to keep as a sports writer. He was a beautiful man who dearly loved the beautiful game, and he will be missed. Think about it...

Think about it..

April 3, 2014

Nēnē Neighbors

According to a recent report, a pair of nēnē geese has arrived on O'ahu and is apparently raising a brood of three little ones. This gaggle of geese came from the Big Island and arguably stopped off on O'ahu's north shore on their way to Kaua'i, possibly to enjoy some fresh Kahuku corn or savory shrimp. Why they choose to stop here is causing the Twitter universe, Pinterest, and Facebook circles to go crazy. This might even beat a piano-playing cat! After all, this nēnē sighting is considered a first on O'ahu since the 1700s, which was a few years before social networking began.

If it is true that nēnē have been avoiding O'ahu for about 300 years, it's big news. Local visitor bureau marketers are sure to want to capitalize on this new breed of tourist to help out in those tumultuous periods when we see visitor drop-off from the mainland US or Japan. And these visitor don't require expanded airline lift, a real plus. Apparently, the nēnē has become a better flying machine, new and improved through Darwinian intervention, and thus a stopover on O'ahu is simply no longer necessary like it was in the good old days before nēnē got into yoga, weight lifting, and watched their diets. Efforts to save the endangered nēnē have been going on for years, and this visit is yet one more positive sign that the state bird is coming back from the verge of extinction 50 years ago.

Much like the respect people are asked to show with our native honu and monk seals, going near the nēnē is a no-no. This celebrity couple and their kids should be treated like the Hollywood types that frequent our shores. It's OK to look from afar, but let's just leave them alone and let them enjoy some quality family time. Hopefully, they'll get visits from other friends and family, and O'ahu will appear back on the radar screen of this long-missing famous fowl friend. Think about it...

Habitat loss, predation, and local vehicular collisions are still sad realities for nēnē in the wild. Alas, O'ahu is once again nēnē-less, unfortunately, as this family saga did not end up with a happy, fairy-tale ending. The nēnē parents on O'ahu passed away in 2015, and only one gosling survived over the ensuing years. He was subsequently moved to a Big Island nēnē sanctuary in 2019 after touring O'ahu for a few years.

April 10, 2014

When Things Take Forever

To say vital projects sometimes move slowly in Hawai'i would be an understatement. While we cherish our more leisurely pace of life here, sometimes it precludes getting things done. Projects take longer than planned to finish at real cost and its often treated like no big deal. As the completion nears for the Clarence T. C. Ching Athletics Complex on UH's lower campus, an assessment of why there were delays of one year and a $3 million overage on costs was somehow deflected by suggestions that there could have been better communication along the way.

Really? Adults in charge who saw the clock ticking and costs rising couldn't figure that out before the NCAA got concerned and ultimately the costs rose $3 million over budget and the project took an extra 12 months to complete? But apparently, that's just another "whatevah." We've gotten good or perhaps just numb here in simply accepting dysfunction like this. Another example of our passive nature came when I read just how little has been done to create the vital infrastructure needed to allow Kalaeloa (formerly Barbers Point Naval Air Station) to grow and prosper. Oh yeah, the Navy moved out 15 years ago.

The city of Honolulu and state of Hawai'i can't get together on basics like roadways and sewer issues, according to an eye-opening article in Pacific Business News. One city official was quoted as saying, "In a way, it's nobody's fault." He went on to then place blame on rules in place today. Rules made by people in charge at some point. And so Kalaeloa, like the Waikīkī natatorium, Blaisdell Arena, and the windward Stairway to Heaven continue to devolve because not enough people care to resolve issues, make decisions, and move forward. When things move a bit slowly here ostensibly to ensure they're done right, that's sold as common sense and sensible caution. But far too often, things simply don't get done due to bureaucratic intransigence, lack of passion, and covering-one's-butt syndrome. It's not a pretty side of paradise. Think about it...

Nice to know that nowadays we've evolved such that we never have major projects go over cost, over deadline, or without constant rancor and butt-covering excuse making...

Think about it.

May 12, 2014

Jury Justice

If you've ever been summoned to appear for jury duty, the first three thoughts that might go through your mind are: Why me? I don't have time for this. How can I get off from this time-consuming function? Well, think again. Beyond the simple fact that it is a civic duty to sit on a jury of peers unless there are compelling reasons to ask to be dismissed, the actual process is fascinating and revealing.

I recently sat in the jury box for a circuit court case that stretched out over four days due to recesses and days off for various reasons. I found the instructions from the articulate judge to be clear, helpful, and thought-provoking. While we all bring our own personal baggage and beliefs into any subjective situation, you hope that the facts, as laid out by lawyers, witnesses, and/or defendants, will provide you with enough information to make a rational, objective decision that leaves you clear in mind and conscience, without a reasonable doubt.

My fellow jurors provided articulate rationale and spoke with conviction as we deliberated behind closed doors to come up with our verdict. People who I'd never seen before and perhaps will never see again shook off the dysfunctional nature of midday jury calls, 90-minute lunches, and mediocre attorney questioning to render a decision, and did so with an absolute seriousness that belied the nervous nature of being in court, speaking up among strangers, and making decisions about someone else's future. So the next time you get that simple civic request in the mail, hopefully it will remind you that this legal proceeding helps to define what a true democracy is all about. It may be an inconvenience, but it's most certainly a necessary one here in Hawai'i and throughout this democratic country. Think about it...

Excuse making...

May 15, 2014

Jack Be Nimble

A couple of weeks ago I proclaimed that Bruno Mars was already arguably Hawai'i's most successful musical export of all time. Well, let me backtrack a bit and give some props to a gentleman who is right up there with the Mars man, and that's Jack Johnson. Not only does Johnson continually hit the top of the charts with his CDs and songs, but he also does things in a helpful yet humble and cool way as he meanders along.

His recent effort to ensure that local fans got to buy tickets for his upcoming August 1 Waikiki Shell concert before scalpers and others jumped in was a class move. His appearance at Mililani Ike Elementary School last week was yet another example of his subtle, laid-back, yet valuable efforts to entertain and educate, as he spoke about his Kōkua Hawai'i Foundation and his pitch to focus on the environmental three Rs—reduce, reuse, and recycle. Not complex, but surely noteworthy and not heavy-handed or objectionable. The foundation's recycling efforts in Hawai'i's classrooms have doubled in size, as 29 schools now actively participate.

What a concept, doing good by doing things well in an entertaining manner. Mililani Ike actually earned Johnson's singing appearance by doing a great job recycling bottle caps. Teaching our keiki that it's cool to be conscious of our environment by taking simple steps to help ensure a greener future is yet another example of Johnson's genuine jones to make a difference. And when it comes to making a difference locally and elsewhere, Jack's at the top of the charts. Long may he reign as he helps eliminate acid rain. Instead of just "sitting, waiting, wishing," Johnson continues to prove that he's not some "flake," but rather is "good people" who's making things "better together" because there's "no other way." P.S. Those are a few of his song titles...think about it.

Bruno is now bigger than ever, and Jack continues to give back locally as he does his thing.

Full Disclosure Dysfunction

Transparency and accountability concerns won out over logic last week when a new law went into effect that requires persons serving on more than a dozen state boards to fully disclose the financial interests of their entire family. The obvious impact of this law was the immediate resignation of at least 18 people from boards including the University of Hawai'i regents, Land & Natural Resources, the Land Use Commission, and the Hawaii Housing Finance & Development Corporation. In essence, the law says the rights of the people to know your personal financial information outweigh your individual right to privacy.

And that's a sticky wicket, because the logical premise that drove this legislation is that conflicts of interest can be more easily ascertained in advance of decisions through exposing one's complete financial records. But dig a little deeper, and you'll find that apparently the Ethics Commission, which supported the bill through its legislative approval process, finds it is overwhelmed by a vast amount of paperwork that it simply can't handle with its current limited staffing, and this inability to vet paperwork helped push through the resolution.

If that's the major issue here—not enough help to do myriad, detailed financial examinations well and on a timely basis—then why wasn't a solution suggested that adds two or three more administrators to the Ethics Commission to ensure a timely flow of paperwork with information that would be thorough, yet sealed and kept confidential, as is already done with information on thousands of other state employees, board members, and commissioners? The heavy-handed decision in this situation resulted in some really good, civic-minded citizens feeling compelled to resign from boards, and many more will now be reluctant to volunteer for these important committees. We'll never know how many shy away because they simply won't apply to give of their time and valuable input, and that's a shame and surely not serving the public interest, is it? Think about it...

Think about it

Weather or Not

So how prepared were you this past week? How much forethought did you give to the wild weather that was presumed to be coming our way? Did you think beyond a day or two after the onset of wind and rain? Did you have plans for keeping medication refrigerated if the power was out for a week, if that's an issue for you? Did you think about getting to and caring for a disabled or elderly family member living in a high-rise? Did you have enough pet food if the stores were closed? Did you think about being forced to stay home due to trees being down or roads being flooded for a few days?

Or, did you passively look at this double hurricane whammy approaching and say ho hum? Did you calmly prognosticate that nothing would happen, because the last time wild winds threatened, nothing really bad happened, and the last few tsunami warnings saw just minor ripples on our shores? Sure, you can roll the dice and underprepare; you can avoid stocking up on the basics, like water, batteries, a portable radio, and easy-to-prepare foods.

But what happens when we do get hit really hard? What if you have no electricity and the harbors are damaged, so there are no food deliveries, no credit cards can be used, no running water, no public services, no work, no salaries, no easy access to 30-story condos, no refrigeration for medical supplies, etc., etc.? Are you really ready? Or are you just going to continue to make assumptions based on our past good fortune? And what might the price be for complacency or "ainokea"? This last nature warning might give you reason to do more than just think about it...

This one rings true every year here, come hell or (more probably) high water.

Rental Reboot

Whoops. The Hawaii Tourism Authority just completed a study showing there may be as many as 26,500 houses and condos being used for vacationers or short-term rental. While the final figures are being tabulated before official release to the public, this reported figure of 26,900 units is quite a bit higher than the previously released figure of 6,900...by almost 20,000 more units.

The report says there are now 4,478 such units on Oʻahu—the previous number reported was 555. Oahu has not permitted short-term usage permits in 25 years. Hmmmm... And on Maui, where the number was thought to be about 3,342 units, there are now apparently 11,166 units. And while Maui does still have a permit process, how many of these just-realized units do you think are actually accounted for in city or state tax records? How many of these units are in areas zoned as residential? How many neighbors find it strange that 15 different people come and go from the unit or house next door over the course of an average year? How many local people can't find reasonable rentals in the same areas due to the simple math that it's easier to charge a premium to 15 different guests over the course of a year than to charge one long-term renter?

When the new, official numbers come out pertaining to short-term rental units, someone should explain how the figures could have been so far off for years, and then someone in the enforcement world should tell us how this growing dilemma will be dealt with. Legal units that provide a more local experience for visitors might be fine, but only if they are bona fide, accounted for legal units, with all of the taxes and regulations that go along with them. Let's have that discussion based on facts. As we regularly hear of the need for more relatively affordable housing units for locals, let's get a reality check on the hidden world of vacation rentals.

Now here is one that has been addressed, at least in form. We'll see how the crackdown goes, and then we'll see how real estate prices go, all because we waited far too long for action of some sort.

Think about it

The Gift of Life

Having a baby is one of the most exciting, intimate, and amazing experiences a human being can have. But did you know that there's a way for you to help make it even more fulfilling? The Hawaii Cord Blood Bank is a repository for a baby's umbilical cord blood unit, which is most often discarded upon birth. By making the conscious choice to allow the hospital to save this vital, life-giving cord blood, you can help to save a life. Yes, something that would normally be discarded, can help save a life.

Persons suffering from life-threatening disorders like leukemia and lymphoma have already been helped by the Hawaii Cord Blood Bank. Working in conjunction with the Puget Sound Blood Center, seven cord blood units recently collected right here in Hawai'i helped to save lives, bringing the total units used thus far from Hawai'i to over 150. All you need to do is elect to allow the hospital you give birth in to work in conjunction with the Hawaii Cord Blood Bank. The cord is discarded as medical waste if parents do not opt to donate. There are private collection options, too, if you so choose.

Cord blood units donated through the Hawaii Cord Blood Bank—check it out at www.hcbb.org—are registered with the National Bone Marrow Registry and thus the incredible gift of life becomes available internationally. Saving a life while creating a life—what a concept, and so easy to do, simply by allowing the medical experts to not discard the valuable life-saving cord blood. For those about to give birth, this simple act of selflessness can make a landmark day even better for someone you don't even know, and what a story to tell your keiki in the years to come. Think about it...

Think about it.

Boys to Men

All of this talk recently about the NFL, HPD, and the problems of domestic violence and physical abuse have led some to posture that perhaps some good will come of these high-profile incidents, that perhaps people will now address these issues seriously. Well, that just doesn't cut it. We've known about and heard about domestic abuse and physical violence for decades, and one solid way to act on the issue to help ensure that this trend doesn't continue generation after generation is to educate and mentor the young.

The same way we must teach our kids about better eating habits and healthy ways to grow their minds and bodies, we need to stop the trend that often times seems genetic: bad role models, bad family history, etc. Well, good news, there are steps in place to educate our keiki. One good example is Ala Kuola, a nonprofit entity that runs a year-old program called Coaching Boys to Men, which came from the Future Without Violence entity in California. It's an athletics-based program that aims to reduce dating violence and future domestic violence by training coaches to be positive role models who deliver a series of violence prevention messages to their young student athlete as part of their regular training program. This is not a one-day or one-month cram course; these are life lessons requiring repetition, sincerity, integrity, and strength of conviction.

Positive attitudes toward women, respect for relationships (casual and more intimate) for all people—whether in person or on social media (and that includes no bullying), and the fact that there is no excuse for abuse...period. Violence shows weakness, not strength, and Ala Kuola is helping to make that point without being heavy-handed. We need more hands-on lessons like this effort to reverse this troubling trend. Why should we be surprised when video shows us what we all know exists? Domestic abuse, child abuse, taunting, bragging—it's gotta go. Ala Kuola is a great example of action being taken now and it needs to be promoted and utilized throughout this state more often for more people to experience. There's no excuse for abuse, and no excuse for pretending this phenomenon just showed up last month. We need to act now for the future. Think about it...

"We need to act now for the future" was the last line in this five-year-old editorial. And the future brought us the "Me Too" movement. Thankfully...

Signing Off

It is sign waving season as we head toward the November general election. Yeh! Scores of local politicians and their supporters are taking to the streets to try to get us to believe they can make a difference in our worlds by holding up signs and distracting us as we drive. It's hard enough eating, reading, and texting when I drive, so having the faithful standing just off the streets on your behalf is really something that many voters really don't need or value.

I recently saw two signs for politicians that featured the candidates' complete family. At 35 mph, I really wasn't able to clearly delineate the details of the family photo, but I don't really think I'm going to cast my vote based on who has the nicer family portrait or makes a stronger fashion statement. Frankly, I'd rather see the politicos' sign wavers holding messages with some details about how you're going to fix things—in big letters. Or drop off a simple pamphlet with detailed plans for our future that might encourage voters. And here's a thought, rather than crowd 50 people into a one-block area that's heavily trafficked (as if that shows me that you have huge support), why not spread the loyal sign holders out over a larger area—thus giving me the subliminal impression that you must be good, because you're everywhere?!

And this bit about standing out there in the rain, smiling and waving—I'm not sure if I'm sold on the assumption that this shows me how tough and dedicated you are, or rather that you're simply too silly and caught up in the long campaign to know to come out of the rain. Luckily, it is easier than ever to find out details about what the candidates really think and plan to do, and that's our job as voters. So, some of us simply sigh at silly sign waving, an archaic local political season custom. It might actually distract or detract—and surely that's not a politician's goal. Maybe it's time to sign off. Think about it...

October 20, 2014

A Gift for the Ages

   Fresh off last week's editorial about UH Mānoa's mounting debt comes a huge piece of good news. By giving the University of Hawai'i leased fees on various land parcels, housing big-time buildings in Chicago, Charlotte, Nashville, and Columbus, Ohio, philanthropist and savvy UH graduate Jay Shidler will be increasing his total donations to the University of Hawai'i Shidler Business College to over $100 million. That's phenomenal! He's UH's first ever $100 million donor, and the gift and confidence it shows says as much about UH as it does about Mr. Shidler.

   For here's an entrepreneur who has done well who has now decided to do even more good for his alma mater. Shidler began the gift giving in earnest about 10 years ago with a $25 million offering, followed by $6 million for renovations. And these lease fees from the mainland will provide almost $70 million, which will allow UH to do the following, according to the Shidler College of Business Vision: expand programs and academic support, increase internships and career opportunities, provide more scholarships to more students, increase faculty endowments, improve facilities, recruit world-class faculty, attract top students from all over, increase national and international perception of the business school, provide study abroad opportunities...the list goes on and on. A great vision that will now be realized through a great gift that will keep on giving.

   And this giving, at a time of great need for UH, will perhaps stimulate other well-to-do UH alumni to come forward and help UH achieve even more, perhaps in other academic areas. With UH's revenue streams from tuition and the legislature slowing down annually, this gift is exactly what UH needs in its quest to move forward, and that is the surely the hope and expectation of Jay Shidler. Mr. Shidler has put his money where his Hemi is, and that's a great example of leadership and passion that hopefully leads to copycats who join him soon in the UH philanthropic hall of fame. Think about it...

Think about it.

October 23, 2014

Lahaina E-merges

In case you missed it last week, Google named Lahaina as this year's city for the state of Hawai'i, meaning that the Maui town is the "strongest online business" community of any city in our state and is helping to pave the way down the digital highway. It's a nice accolade from the internet giant, but one problem with Google's announcement was the fact that Google misspelled the word

"Lahaina" five times throughout its press release, which extolled the city's connectivity and business savvy. A quote in the Google release from Maui mayor Alana Arakawa did have the correct spelling of Lahaina, as you might expect. Apparently, no one in-house caught that at Google.

So yes, Google is human after all, just like that little bald man behind the curtain in The Wizard of Oz, and some marketing Googler apparently didn't notice the spelling error from the headline down into the fine print. Perhaps archaic tools such as spell check or proofreading would have helped. Being well thought of and well connected online might be no more significant anywhere else in this country outside of isolated Hawai'i. With our unique culture and one-of-a-kind product offerings, the web is oftentimes a local retailer's only method of reaching a wider base of potential shoppers. Obviously, very few shoppers simply pull off the highway to browse on their way through in Hawai'i as mainland folks do when traveling interstate or intra-continent. Google says 97 percent of internet users look online for products and services. Some users also look for correct spelling.

The undoubtedly tech savvy Google bungler who fumbled the spelling of Lahaina should know that Lahaina means "cruel sun" or "merciless sun" in Hawaiian, and misspelling the name of a city that you are awarding recognition to is surely cruel and unusual punishment, so that's why I'm dedicating this merciless editorial to the all-powerful Google, which is so big and well positioned now that it has become a verb in our lexicon, like Xerox and FedEx. When we verb-ify companies or products, we probably expect excellence or at least certain high standards, and Google's boo-boo by not using its noodle points out that even omnipotence comes at a cost. Think about it...

A Wonder from Hawai'i

On Monday, the late Patsy Mink will receive the highest civilian honor offered in this country—the Presidential Medal of Freedom. Mink's story should be made into a movie, and her tale, along with Dr. Donnis Thompson at DH, is the basis for the wonderful Rise of the Wahine documentary, which has just been released. Denied entry into medical school due to her gender, Mink made a mockery of the inequalities she saw around her and changed things for good with her authorship of the landmark Title IX gender equity education bill. Mink was a visionary and a hero, rising from humble Maui roots to become the first ever non-Caucasian female elected to serve in this nation's Congress.

Along with Mink, the great Stevie Wonder will be honored with the presidential medal on Monday. So I thought it might be fun to look through Wonder's incredible catalogue of songs and apply some of his song titles that aptly represent or mirror the quest of Ms. Mink. How about "Hold On to Your Dream," "I Ain't Gonna Stand for It," or "I Wish"? Then there's "Isn't She Lovely," "Justice of the Heart," "More Than a Dream," and the emphatic "Signed, Sealed, Delivered I'm Yours." Add in "Somebody Knows, Somebody Cares," "Something to Say," "Superwoman (Where Were You When I Needed You)," and finish it off with "You Can't Judge a Book By Its Cover" from Wonder's amazing repertoire, and it is truly wonderful to see these two legends from different worlds being honored for their contributions to our nation at the same time.

As we look around in search of difference makers and heroes of today and tomorrow, the acknowledgment of the efforts and passion of Patsy Mink in Washington, DC, on Monday is a fitting tribute to a daughter of these islands who literally looked up, saw the need for drastic change, and then made it happen. As I'm sure Stevie would admit, she was a "Golden Lady." Think about it...

Think about it

Drone Moan

Look, up in the sky...it's a bird, it's a plane...actually, it's a creepy drone. Yes, the drone moan has begun, and it's happening right here on Kaua'i, as locals are starting to get riled about flying cameras above them while they try to relax in privacy or swim without being burdened by unwanted and unnecessary whirlybirds from above.

It's really only a matter of time before injury is caused—a drone taking pictures it shouldn't, a drone diving on to someone's head due to malfunction or pilot error, a drone getting too close to the airport somewhere. And those would just be mistakes, not problems due to malicious intent. Those days are coming, too. Good luck having the police try to police the skies for these noisy, insects-on-steroids, invasive, clunky gizmos. Drones can be great for gathering scenic footage, mapping hard-to-get-at areas and agricultural fields, providing vital military information, and even for delivering essential supplies.

But it would be naïve to not see the great danger—to our privacy and to our health—that these unmanned mechanical sky hawks might pose as they become more prevalent, less costly, and easier to obtain and fly. So while Kaua'i residents have raised an early caution and concern, it sadly won't be the last. Nor should it be. The FAA should have regulations in place within a year. Drones, like syringes and the internet, can provide good, but can easily be misused for nefarious purposes, and we'll see how technology, personal space, and personal freedom clash in the years to come in Hawai'i and elsewhere as we all get buzzed. Think about it...

Drones thankfully haven't yet taken over our skies. But with any new technology comes abusers, so let's hope the creeps, voyeurs, and safety-last delivery types stay below the radar and the horizon.

Think about it.

January 22, 2015

Tortoise Among Us

A wayward tortoise was found in the driveway of a Kāneʻohe homeowner last week. It turns out that the turtle belonged to the next-door neighbor, but an awful lot of people came forward, claiming that the tortoise was theirs. Others simply called in and said they would be happy to house the turtle. Of course, the turtle itself provided no comment, nor do we know if the turtle was actually trying to escape, as speed is not often an indication of a turtle's real motives.

With all of this activity and commotion, I fear this tortoise is becoming a mere shell of what he or she used to be. Perhaps the wandering turtle could be loaned for a short time to the legislature to show it as an analogy of something that moves slowly and appears lost. State agriculture officials determined the tortoise's owner when the next-door neighbor came forward, though the creature indicated that he avoids Facebook and Twitter like the plague and has also refused repeated tattoo attempts, except for the "ainokea" one.

To help boost attendance at the first UH home football game next fall, some have suggested a race between the tortoise and a rabbit, but that sounds harebrained to me, so let's just support our team because it's our team. Logic always indicated that either this tortoise came from a home nearby to where he was found or he's been a road warrior for years, living off the lush underbrush. Perhaps he simply missed the bus and was taking a shortcut. Now that he's been reunited with his owners, he can live the next 125 years or so in peace, as yes, tortoises can live that long, which might be an indication that we should all just slow down and enjoy the ride. Think about it...

February 19, 2015

Kidney Care

Organ donations. A touchy subject, especially in Hawai'i. There are about 450 people on the kidney transplant waiting list in Hawai'i, which makes Hawai'i the highest per capita state for the need for donors. At times, nearly one in three people on that list here is a child, some of whom won't make it to adulthood without a transplant.

Kidney donations from live donors have dwindled in Hawai'i over the past decade, and the need for exact matching donors with our genetic bouillabaisse sometimes means that we can't wait for kidneys from afar, compounded by the fact that mainland medical transplant teams don't want to risk the long flight required to send us out-of-state donations. With fewer traumatic deaths here than elsewhere, there are simply fewer available kidneys in general for transplant purposes.

Hawai'i has a high rate of diabetes and hypertension, both destroyers of kidneys, so sadly the need here will remain high. Transplanted kidney recipients from living donors tend to live twice as long as recipients from deceased donors. The laparoscopic donor surgery allows the lifesaving giver to go home in a day or two, as the donor's other healthy kidney takes over complete kidney functions. The donor pays nothing for his or her efforts. And if a donor should ever need a kidney, he or she moves to the top of the transplant list because they gave of themselves in such a huge way to help save another person's life. No, it's not for everyone. It is a life-changing event, for everyone involved. It gives real meaning to the term "lifesaver." It's your call, of course, and perhaps an opportunity for you to think about it...

There are now approximately 271 people on the local kidney transplant waiting list, which is a far more detailed and qualified list than the list we had in 2015. Per capita, Hawai'i remains number one nationally in need of transplant donors. Not good... You can help out or simply find out more by calling (808) 593-1515. Make a difference, however you feel comfortable...

April 2, 2015

College Counts

A recent report notes that more Hawai'i high school students are college bound these days, up about 11 percent over the college matriculation rate of local students five years ago. About 56 percent of our high school seniors head off to college, in spite of recent surveys and articles that question the overall value of college and its cost burdens. But here's one thing no report based on pure numbers will point out. College is far more than an academic exercise. If a quality life is partly reflected by having options and choices as you go along, then it is hard to argue that increased education—knowing more stuff about more stuff—provides an individual with more confidence and greater options about where to go next or what to do next in life.

How many people in their 20s, 30s, or 40s lament not having made better use of their high school days? How many now realize that perhaps, just perhaps, they might have had more avenues to explore, which might have led to greater financial flexibility and more ability to seek alternative careers, if only they had worked a little harder or striven to get to the next level during those turbulent teen years.

College is not for everyone. And everyone who goes to college does not take full advantage of the opportunity afforded them. Having more options, choices, and knowledge is a plus when it comes to choosing a career rather than feeling forced into a job. Being happy in what you do sure beats simply showing up every day, just like in a personal relationship—and education is one piece of the puzzle to help give you a confidence edge and a sense of accomplishment. Here's hoping that the Hawai'i college numbers continue to climb. Think about it...

The numbers of high school grads here who immediately go on to college has not moved in six years (about 56 percent still), partially due to a burgeoning job market, perhaps. But for future opportunities and choices in careers, college still makes sense for those so inclined.

May 4, 2015

Homelessness vs. Helplessness?

We're not winning the war on homelessness, much like we have never won the war on drugs or poverty. But rather than just talk about talking about the situation, what can be done to make a concrete, realistic, analytically defined difference? Rather than just shuffle the homeless around from the leeward beaches to 'A'ala Park to Kaka'ako and Waikīkī as we've done for 30 years, what steps can be taken to immediately help alleviate this problem/crisis? And while there is no single or simple answer, we need more people involved, not talking.

What if more medical professionals, doctors, and mental health experts volunteered to help the understaffed professionals already trying to deal with homeless individuals and made case-by-case assessments? There are plenty of people in the local psychology field helping out already, but is there a concerted effort to create a system whereby it would be easy for trained professionals to contact someone and provide intervention immediately? Is there a clearinghouse that makes it easier for willing medics, able to give of their time, to get into contact with people most in need? What if other 250 medical professionals, beyond the already helpful Veterans Administration, came forward to provide much-needed analysis and directed people who truly do want answers? Could that begin to help reduce numbers by 100 or more in the coming months?

Treating people in need simply as Good Samaritans by extending their Hippocratic Oath beyond daily private practices would be a real plus in the ongoing effort to make a difference on our streets. But there needs to be coordination. Here's another thought: Salt Lake City's Housing First initiative has reduced chronic homelessness there by 72 percent; have we looked hard at that option? I know housing in general is hard to come by in Hawai'i. But with more public–private efforts, the time is right for absolute action and some restraint on political pontifications with minimal results. We need action and we need it now. Think about it...

"We need action and we need it now." Oh, I said that four years ago. Well, perhaps "now" is a relative term locally. A few ideas have sprouted action, but more has to be done.

 **Think** about it.

May 21, 2015

Nursing Home Nonsense: A Real Story

The "system" doesn't work for Noboru and Elaine Kawamoto. They are a local couple who've been married for 67 years and now both need help through foster care. But the system doesn't allow two private-paying clients to be housed in a community care foster family home as there needs to be space available for Medicaid clients. That's the law. The legislature had a chance to fix this seemingly correctable rule, but it did nothing. Perhaps the rule could have been amended to allow for two private care patients along with two Medicaid patients in one home, or four Medicaid patients in one home. That's what House Bill 600 proposed. And it never got out of committee. So this couple, together for 67 years in matrimony, is now kept apart due to the system, a system based on the law that was ostensibly created so that people who could not afford private home care could still find a place to be taken care of.

But to keep a married couple apart...well that's just not right. So rather than wait for eight months until the legislature is back in session, is there anyone in officialdom who can help a couple who've been married since the 1950s get back together again in Kāneʻohe, their preferred home, and not just on weekends when beleaguered family members can drive them back and forth? House Bill 600 might have had its flaws, in which case it should have been tweaked, or maybe there are some other reasons that involved legislators didn't like its contents. Maybe some outside, high-powered players didn't like its intent and convinced elected officials to quash it. Who knows? Certainly all bills cannot be passed for every individual circumstance that exists outside the system, whatever system is in question. But a system that deprives a married couple from living together? Come on, somebody fix this. Think about it...

In Hawaiʻi facilities at all levels for the aging and aged (palliative care, hospice care, geriatric nursing) will continue to be a growing issue over the next 25 years.

June 15, 2015

Oxymorons and False Truths

Last week some false killer whales showed up off the Kona coast, and while it was great to see this unique excursion, it got me thinking about the plight of these majestic creatures. How'd you like to go through your whole life being called "false." If these dolphins are having an identity problems, it's because we've misnamed them. Known formally as Pseudorca crassidens, why do we keep calling them false anything; let's call them by their real name. No one calls anyone a false genius, but they surely might label them an idiot.

Here's another one badly mislabeled: jumbo shrimp. Come on, if they're shrimp, they simply can't be jumbo. Shrimp implies little, puny, and if these behemoths of the shrimp world deserve more serious recognition well, then let's give it to 'em! How about "royal shrimp"? I know, shrimp refers to the entity as a form of crustacean, not its size, but it just doesn't feel right. And how about our very own pineapple, which is neither pine nor apple? Spaniards thought it looked like a pinecone, and the English apparently likened its juicy fruit to apples—simple, but so wrong. How about thorny fruit, or prickly pod?

Here's another one: uncontested divorce—well, someone's a bit upset? Paid volunteers? Pretty ugly? Original copy? Or a classic civil war—nothing civil about war, is there? We have a number of these oxymorons well represented here—stay/go is a good one. Well, as I always say amidst the confusion on many things in life locally and elsewhere—if can, can; if no can, no can. Think about it...

Think about it...

Fix It

A 30 year old man broke his ankle last week trespassing in the wee hours of the morning while trying to get to—you guessed it, the Haʻikū Stairs, otherwise known as the Stairway to Heaven. This is no real surprise, actually, it's symptomatic of the bureaucratic slipping up that's gone on far too long on this issue. It has always been just a matter of time before we hear of a major injury, a tense stand-off with neighbors, or something more serious, but this incident does remind us that many more months have passed since the last episode of As the World Stands Still as various state and city branches of government still haven't committed to a definitive plan to either upgrade, reconfigure, or destroy theses storied steps.

And just like you've heard here before, it is often easier to not make a decision, to not risk alienating any people (aka voters and constituents), to not finalize plans and set a definitive time line for action. It's not just the Stairway to Heaven that gets discussed ad nauseam with no action or plan, it's also the Waikīkī World War I natatorium; it's the issue of ramping up solar while the electric company's revenues go down; it's the constant disrepair at Honolulu Airport and many public parks and their facilities; it's the lack of air and books in local classrooms...the list goes on.

Perhaps it's a lack of leadership, a lack of willingness to take a stand, a lack of conviction due to covering one's political ʻōkole, but whatever it is, it's pervasive and it's doing no one a favor here—not our citizens, elected officials, or perception from afar as to how Hawaiʻi works, or doesn't work. Decisions on issues with disparate viewpoints are never simple as some group will always feel slighted, ignored, or betrayed, but decisions have to be made at some point, don't they? So who will step forward and fix some of these things? Who will step up on the Haʻikū steps? And who will demand that decisions are made if not the people? Get up, stand up, stand up for your right. Action time has come, on something. Think about it...

Unresolved, overstudied issues like this make snarky editorial writing a breeze sometimes...sadly.

July 6, 2015

Ethics-shhh; Homeless-zzzz

So much to talk about and so little time. How about the Honolulu Ethics Commission, which acted unethically by putting a muzzle on its executive director and staff? If the commission has issues with information being disseminated, then deal with it internally and respond, don't tell the public, which deserves to hear the opinions of those in charge of keeping an eye on our elected officials, that we will no longer be served, that every utterance will be vetted, and that an official's public disagreement or statement is tantamount to treason. There's a fine lesson in civics, kids. Ask no questions, because we'll give you no answers.

On another note, the repetitious whack-a-mole mentality of forcing the homeless to relocate from time to time is a losing battle. It causes frustration on all sides, and points out the immediate need to find intermediate housing options on Sand Island and elsewhere. This is not a new problem locally, it's just growing, and some estimates are that the number of homeless people statewide is larger than official figures currently indicate. From 'A'ala Park in the 1990s to O'ahu's leeward beaches 15 years ago, homeless residents have found a way to survive wherever they've been moved from. From the shores of the Kapālama Canal to the side streets around the Children's Discovery Center in Kaka'ako, from the sit-lie restricted areas to the constant sight of three HPD cars pulled over as officers address a lone vagrant, we all see the tarps and tents and problems—every day.

Government forces at the city and state level need to work better together regularly to offer solutions—not theories, not social statements, and not empty promises. We know where these people cannot be. We need an answer as to where they can and should be, at least on an interim basis with a goal of mainstreaming them and getting them help as needed. These people are homeless, not hopeless. As solutions do finally arise from the slow processes in place, at least we'll get to question officials, something we'll apparently no longer get to do with duct taped ethics gurus. Think about it...

Think about it..

July 9, 2015

Legislative Pondering

How many bureaucrats does it take a screw in a light bulb? I don't know, and I certainly don't want to put myself on the line, but let me get a study going on it. Just kidding, but some of you may think that quasi joke really sums up our local legislative process. But is it fair to expect full-time work from part-time employees? After all, our legislature is just like 24 other states' elected officials who are part-time, yet say they devote at least 70 percent of their working hours to their legislative duties. 10 states have full-time elected officials. Some small, rural states meet even fewer days than the 60 working days required in our local bylaws. 60 days! It's summertime, do you know where your representative is?

Would you be satisfied with a part-time doctor or lawyer handling your problems? Would you expect potential conflicts of interest when our 76 legislative elected officials also work in the private sector when they're not toiling on Punchbowl Street? Nebraska has a unicameral and nonpartisan legislature—one legislative body. At least 14 states have approached Nebraska for details on how it works—including Hawai'i, at one point.

While no legislature would ever think to vote itself out of existence, perhaps a full-time, single legislative body here would generate more interest and provide more value to an apathetic, nonvoting public. Perhaps such an entity could completely focus on just the people's issues, not their other jobs that require focus 12 months a year. Do you think it's worth considering? Good, I'll get a study going on it. Think about it...

So if we're still relatively unhappy with the legislative system, where's the push to change it? Ethics of convenience and subtle conflicts of interest simply shouldn't be the norm.

Think about it

August 10, 2015

Ethical Decision

Despite what you may think, the term "good government" is not an oxymoron, like jumbo shrimp, pretty ugly, or original copy. An example of government calling itself out and rectifying a mistake came through loud and clear a couple of weeks back when the Honolulu Ethics Commission rescinded an earlier policy to effectively muzzle its executive director and ethics commissioners.

By admitting its mistake in putting the silly rule in effect in the first place, the ethics commission had earned the deserved wrath of most people with belly buttons in this state. One commissioner was out of state at the time of the original vote, and two others apparently mistook what was being voted on, and thus we now have placid waters whereby the ethics commissioner can freely speak his piece, when called for. As it should be, an entity that is beholden to the general population and that is entrusted to ensure that people in office and in government in general act ethically should be able to come forward to explain opinions without restraint. At the same time, it is not unreasonable to expect the face of that entity to attempt to keep his board apprised in advance of making major public statements, which will be made with the people's interests at heart, one has to hope.

If such leaders put their feet in their mouths, then they should be held accountable for actions and words, just like any other leader whose job partly entails representing a company, public or private. So a wrong has been righted, and an ethical decision on ethics by the ethics commission has effectively cleaned up an earlier oversight or blunder. Kudos to the ethics commission for this mea culpa. If only more entities and elected or appointed individuals thought about what was best for the common folk first, or at least more often than we normally see as egos, power, control, and reelections too often get in the way. Ah, we can dream, can't we? Think about it...

Think about it.

Decision, Decisions

We're studying the efficacy of barriers and access at Laniākea, again. We're studying whether to save, relocate, or start over with an aging Aloha Stadium. We've been studying what to do with the Waikīkī natatorium and with the so-called Stairway to Heaven in the Koʻolau Mountain Range for over two decades. We're studying ideas about dealing with the homeless and addressing responsibilities and respect surrounding the building of the Thirty Meter Telescope on Mauna Kea.

We tend to study, analyze, meet, restudy, and then call for a new commission to analyze on lots of issues in Hawaiʻi. Often, it seems that we don't come to solutions in a timely manner when the only absolute truth is that you're never going to get 100 percent agreement or happiness when decisions are made and people's lives and emotions are tied to those decisions. But decisions must be made, on all of these issues, and many more locally.

That's what leadership is all about. That's what serving the people is about—understanding that some people won't be happy when conclusions are reached and action is taken. That's what people expect from people in charge. Make the tough decisions, carefully. But none of these issues simply go away or have more clarity by just having yet one more study, site visit, assessment, committee, or public forum—all of which should have been done on all of these projects at the get-go and during fact finding. Let's get concrete decisions on many, if not all, of these hanging issues, and be prepared for the repercussions from those who don't get their way. Think about it...

Hey, at least the Aloha Stadium thing is finally moving forward! Not bad, yeah? The other issues mentioned here...still pending.

September 7, 2015

Time Passages

The American Academy of Pediatrics has recommended a start time of 8:30 a.m. for middle schools and high schools. Research has shown that youngsters' brains work better a bit later in the a.m. each day. It has to do with circadian rhythms. Starting school later locally would also afford kids a better opportunity to get the prescribed minimum of eight and a half hours sleep each night.

Unfortunately, and according to TIME magazine, currently 84 percent of states have at least 75 percent of their schools beginning each weekday before 8:30 a.m. Minnesota now starts school at 8:30 a.m. or later, and the report says that 60 percent of students there now get at least eight hours of sleep per night. Starting school later would also ease some local traffic woes. Of course, starting school later here might also mean starting it later in the year, like the good old days when the school year began around Labor Day, which would also eliminate 30 plus days that public school kids now spend in overheated classrooms that aren't drawing enough attention quickly (after 40 years).

Jackson Hole High School in Wyoming shifted its start time to 8:55 a.m., and the number of car crashes involving teenage drivers dropped by 70 percent. A study at the US Air Force Academy showed that freshmen starting classes after 8 a.m. performed better not only in their first classes but throughout the day. Locally, SEEQS Charter School begins its day with physical activity at 8:30 and academics start at 9:20 a.m., and the school finds its student body to be happier and more engaged. It's time to consider time in our public schools, for a number of reasons. Yes, there are correlated consequences with after school activities and learning time hours, but should we really just ignore this concept as yet another idea that's simply too difficult or cumbersome to incorporate locally? Think about it...

Update on pushing forward school start times or seriously discussing: Zzzzzzz.

Ant On and On

I don't know about you, but I'll be partying this weekend to help celebrate the fact that September is—you guessed it—Stop the Ant Month here in Hawai'i. The proclamation was made by Governor Ige to help remind homeowners and landlords to keep the pesky critters from taking over or at least making their lives uncomfortable, something ants have been trying to do for an estimated 100 million years. And surely fire ants and other crawlers are no laughing matter, but as we celebrate Stop the Ant Month in true anti-ant fashion with parties and fond recollections of kitchen cabinet invasions and dog food incursions, we might consider a few other months to celebrate nontraditional events locally, because any time is a good time to celebrate, right?

How about a Stop the Leaks Month, to remind officials to check our aging infrastructure to prevent the seemingly nonstop sewer line and water main breaks. Yes, we have old lines, but perhaps more coordination to test in advance could preclude some problems. How about a Transparency Month for all elected officials? "Transparency" is a word thrown about just as much as "transgender" these days, and there surely is great value to having at least one month where we actually have transparency in what goes on, like how favors get repaid, and not just lip service or campaign rhetoric come October of every even year.

How about a Keiki Education Month, where we actually resolve age-old issues like providing books for everyone, getting cooler air and working restrooms in our schools, instead of just talking about it annually. Yes, we know you care. But we'd have to see real action taken in Keiki Education Month. So celebrate Stop the Ant Month with your loved ones and friends, and keep those darned critters at bay. But remember, simple awareness isn't the proper answer to all that ails us...action is. Think about it...

"Action" is defined locally as "that which rarely occurs in a timely manner." And "timely" often means "within a decade," locally.

September 21, 2015

A Sporting Stance

How hard is it to simply do the right thing? I don't mean when there is some subjectivity about what's right, but when you know for sure. People in Hawai'i have big hearts—we usually take care of one another. Recently, a business acquaintance of mine was holding a sports tournament and just before the annual event, he found out that someone he has known for six years has a special needs child. He just found out. So, he decided, unbeknownst to that child's parents, to make his tournament a fundraiser for a special child. He decided to act on what he learned. He decided to make a difference because he could, and because he cared.

He put up a banner at the tournament site announcing that the event was to help support this child, and he raised funds over a single weekend, selling T-shirts, including a glass jar where tournament participants and friends could chip in a few dollars extra. In that one weekend alone, he raised $4,000 for the beleaguered family, a family that never complains nor asks for help, a family that no one playing in the event even knew.

When I asked him, he said he did it because his wife always told him to give, no matter what, and to give until it hurts. To give because it's the right thing to do, because everyone who can lend a hand must lend a hand, or an idea, or a check. Those fortunate enough to be in a position to make a difference must make a difference, on some level. And it doesn't just have to be during holiday season. Because you see, for this family, Christmas came in a surprise gift of sharing and love, in September, from a class man full of aloha, humanity, and humility. That concept is surely something we can all act on here as one extended 'ohana; let's not just think about it...

135

Blue Sky Thinking

I was driving over the Koʻolau Mountain Range one glorious morning recently after yet another deluge had literally cleared the air of debris and vog. The sky was a gorgeous blue, and the mountains looked like someone had just chiseled them with a sculptor's knife—jagged peaks interspersed with brilliants shades of green and brown amid the silvery rock. So I did the appropriate and necessary thing and cranked up some music with my windows closed tight. First, my all-time favorite local song, "Kuʻu Home ʻO Kahaluʻu" by Olomana, and then I blasted "The Meeting," by Anderson Bruford Wakeman Howe—the core of the group Yes. Check it out.

Anyway, I actually took the time to be in the moment of real joy and beauty, and I acknowledged how lucky I am on a number of fronts. I don't know when the last time was that you actually took the time to be present when you stand in our aqua waters, slowly scan the horizon while looking out at the ocean or gaze up at the mountains. I don't know if you often or ever reflect on the good things you have going for you, but we surely have the spectacular outdoor opportunities for all for us to just once in a while say, "You know, it's gonna be all right." Attitude can make a big difference in how you deal with things—so maybe, just maybe, look up and around to find your bearing when things are going off kilter.

It's OK to say, "Thank you, Hawaiʻi nei, for being what you are and for allowing me to be here and witness your very essence. And thank you, ears, eyes, mouth, and nose, for giving me sensory capability that I take for granted far too often." Sorry if this sounds a bit ethereal, corny, or schmaltzy, but I thought it might be of some value to think about it...

Think about it

November 23, 2015

Snake Ayes!

So did you hear the one about the guy who was on his way to Costco but never made it because he found a six- to eight-foot snake in his driveway? Actually, that's not a joke, it happened last week on Old Pali Drive, and the homeowner wisely waited until police could arrive to figure out how to corral the serpent into a trash can for delivery back to the state capitol. (Just kidding.)

But eh, no joke, what is it with people who feel the need to smuggle in unwanted, unneeded, and malevolent species? Spiders, snakes, Jackson's chameleons, nonnative aquarium fish, the list goes on and on of entities we don't want and don't need here. Add that to the invasive fire ants, coqui frogs, diurnal mongooses that never did work things out with the nocturnal rats here, and you can see it's just a big mess waiting to happen.

And can it happen here? Well, just ask the folks on Guam how the birds are doing...what birds? The brown tree snakes disrupted that population. Fines and penalties need to be stiff and those delirious daredevils who think bringing contraband animals here is cool and profitable need to be caught and perhaps spend a quiet night in a cell with a hungry boa or a dangerous spider. Inspectors say many of the culprits are locals who can easily find the items they want online or on the mainland, and then smuggle them in. May they be snake bit! Think about it...

Think about it

December 10, 2015

Business vs. Quality of Life

Earlier this year, CNBC ranked all 50 states' business climates, and as you might have guessed, Hawai'i came in dead last. We scored in the bottom 10 percent of all states in workforce, the cost of doing business, infrastructure, cost of living, and education. Overall, West Virginia carne in 49th for best state in which to do business and Rhode Island was ranked 48th. Add to the obvious issue the incessant red tape, bureaucracy, slowness in which things get done, if at all, and it's a wonder to some how anyone could live here, let alone survive or even thrive.

Yet one aspect of this survey taken among business and policy experts, government sources, a CNBC CFO Council and people in the states themselves speak volumes about what keeps it together here. Hawai'i ranks number one in quality of life. That might seem confounding since it's so hard to make ends meet and do business here, but there's simply something about this place that even the toughest critics find enchanting and obviously rewarding. Maybe it's why so many want to visit, just to get a flavor, but not stay here forever.

If you don't believe Hawai'i has a unique or better-than-acceptable quality of life, then does working 10 hours a day, dealing with the worst traffic in America, and overcoming a few other hardships—like the price of milk and housing—make it all worthwhile? I doubt it. So whether you refer to it as our tolerance, aloha spirit, east/west/Polynesia tango, island style—whatever, there is something intangible that keeps us all together far beyond the bottom line. By the way, the top-ranked business states from CNBC? Minnesota is number one, followed by Texas, Utah, Colorado, Georgia, North Dakota, and Nebraska. Thanks, but I'll stay here. Think about it...

Dead last? We need to get a study going on that! Or just go get some 'ono tako poke.

March 28, 2016

Blue Zoo News

The lack of accreditation that the Honolulu Zoo just received is surely a problem. While the general public might not notice a thing, for now, the Association of Zoos and Aquariums accreditation system is an industry-wide insurance policy of sorts for zoos and aquariums. Accreditation makes sure a member meets AZA's standards for animal management and care, including living environments, social groupings, health, and nutrition, according to the AZA website.

Our zoo fell short repeatedly in the financial area—with less than certain assurances year after year about funding and obtaining grants. Immediately at risk for our zoos is up to 10 percent of the zoo's 900 residents, who are here on loan from other zoos. And trust me, if we do lose animals, it won't be the local zoo mongooses or birds. After all, would you want to loan your special and precious animals out to a zoo that might have money problems? Would you risk sending animals to a place that might have care issues if funds don't come in?

On top of this are the seemingly endless repair and maintenance issues and the endless parade of zoo directors—five in the past six years. The Honolulu Zoo needs help, funds, local support, and a plan real soon, or the only bears you might see there down the road will be the empty, or "bare," cages. Hopefully, the promise by those in charge to do better will not be too little, too late for such a worthwhile entity for local and visiting keiki and adults. Like the Pro Bowl, the Sony Open, the Lotte Open, the Ironman Triathlon, and other established draws in Hawai'i, why does it seem like we always wait until threats and drama arise to fix things? Think about it...

It now appears that we have seen some progress, repairs, and a bit more stability. We might not have Dr. Doolittle, but some have done much. More to follow, hopefully.

Think about it

May 30, 2016

Rail Route Reconsideration

Every statement made by new Rapid Transportation board chair Colleen Hanabusa makes her sound more incredulous as to what's going and what had been going on than her last statement as the original and subsequent planning of this project becomes more and more questionable— not necessarily the project, but the plans. Now there's an indication that perhaps Dillingham Boulevard is not the best route to bring the choo choo into town. Really? We're just speculating about that now?! That seems to be a pretty big deal.

Nobody official wants to second-guess the original plans because no one wants to throw the original planners under the bus, or the train, but second-guessing is the game du jour for just about every phase of this plan to link Kapolei with Honolulu via a modern-day transit system. Disruption to drivers and pedestrians in town, ripping up streets to bury electrical lines, the width of the streets, floating deadlines, increased funding needs, the safety of the power lines and Hawaiian Electric repair truck capabilities, overall costs, business disruption and inaccessibility for months if not years, quitting chairpersons—the list of concerns goes on and on, while the train doesn't, and won't, for at least eight more years!

2019 was the originally planned completion date. Then 2022. Now it's 2024. Even the rail's federal cohorts say there's a 35 percent chance the project will not come in at the newly suggested $8.l billion cost. Ya think? But don't worry, as Moe, Larry, and Curly will be brought in shortly to work on engineering, upkeep, and new predictions. Nyuk, nyuk, nyuk. Think about it...

And now it's looking like a rail completion date of 2026, or is that when Halley's Comet returns to our skies?

Think about it

June 2, 2016

Reflecting on the "Good Old Days"

Change is good, as long as it's good change. I hear people lament frequently about how things here and elsewhere have changed, how it's not the "good old days" anymore. Well, that's a relative term, for the good old days in this nation used to mean women stayed home and didn't vote, blacks were slaves, religious persecution was the norm, and due to health conditions and lack thereof, many people died before they were 50 years old.

Locally, the good old days to some surely meant fewer crowds, traffic, hustle and bustle, stress, daily costs, and it meant we saw fewer visitors moving in. But it also meant things like horrible working conditions in the fields, inability of minorities to climb the ruling ranks, and vital goods and services simply didn't make it to our shores or arrived slowly. So as you ponder what the good old days really means to you, also keep in mind the things you, or others, would have to give up, in an imperfect world, in order to have that so-called peace of mind from 30 or 50 or 150 years back.

Yes, hanabata days and nostalgia are often warm and fuzzy—for some. And people here have gotten along and do get along in general far better than in most other places in the land of the free and the home of the brave. But trying to figure out the best way to move things forward for everyone while adhering to some sense of social code—that's the order of the day. That's what our elected officials and leaders need to focus on, both here and in our decaying, vitriolic, cracking nation's capital. Think about it...

Nice to see that things have worked themselves out so well via legislative maturity, empathy, and constructive rapprochement in Washington, DC, eh?

June 23, 2016

Suicide Watch

You might have seen the numbers recently when the 2015 Hawai'i Youth Risk Behavior Survey came out and provided local facts and figures related to teen suicide, drug and alcohol usage, bullying, sexual behavior patterns, etc. Focusing in on the suicide issue, suicide is the second leading cause of death locally for persons aged 15–34. More residents in Hawai'i die by suicide than by homicide annually.

On average, one person dies by suicide every two days here. Suicide is the fifth leading cause of death locally for kids ages 10–14. Hawai'i County is the number one county for suicides locally per capita. Surely this is not just a teen or kids problem, but a problem for all ages here and elsewhere. These numbers are sometimes seen as stark, black and white figures compiled by analysts and statisticians. But they do become far too real for far too many left behind and touched by the horrible emotional loss and ripple effect of this final, desperate act. Education, empathy, a safe haven, awareness, the ability to talk openly and comfort people, trying to stop the incessant hurting; we need to do more.

We need to try and help people come back from the brink—to see the signs of someone feeling desperately sad or hopeless, to see that people are withdrawing or appear to feel helpless. There is no magic answer, and depression and mental illness are hard topics for the layman or ordinary family members to deal with, but we all must do our best and remain conscious of those around us who might be quietly crying out. We need to be brave and forthcoming in attempts to help those who simply can't help themselves. Think about it...

The numbers are updated annually, but they still haunt, stun, and numb us.

Empathy Starts Here

What's the biggest thing a kid needs to learn during the formative years? Well, talk to 10 psychologists, counselors, or sociologists and you might get 10 different opinions. Recently I read a short blurb from one educational psychologist who very strongly suggested that empathy is the most important trait for kids to learn to help ensure their relative happiness and success years later.

Dr. Michele Borba wrote a book called UnSelfie: Why Empathetic Kids Succeed in Our All-About-Me World. The title alone suggests which road we seem to be going down with technology giving us easy access to instant information, a modicum of self-gratification, and an ease with which to say, "Look at what I'm doing," because we all really need to know 24/7. Borba suggests that kids today, thanks in part to technological advances, are more self-absorbed than ever, with narcissism rates up 58 percent in college students vs. 30 years ago. Anecdotal evidence suggests that cheating, bullying, and unhappiness levels are also up among our youth. One bad picture or statement online could peg you forever, in theory. That's a lot tougher than the old word-of-mouth network.

So maybe teaching kindness, awareness of others' needs, and volunteerism will go a long way in your keiki's development. Maybe celebrating helping others more than rigid practice schedules will reap the longer term desired results. As Borba says, "When's the last time you saw a bumper sticker that said 'Proud Parent of a Kind Kid'?" And isn't that what aloha spirit is all about? Making a difference, being kind, humble, and aware. Now to promote these seemingly simple values, the adults must put down their addictive devices, too, of course. Think about it...

Empathy continues to be a sorely lacking human value in 2020.

The Bird's the Word

I would say don't look now, but if you don't look now, you might miss 'em. Apparently, Hawai'i is considered by the American Bird Conservancy to be the "bird extinction capital of the world," according to last month's National Geographic magazine. And that's surely not a nice honorific. According to Nat Geo, only 42 of more than 100 species of birds endemic to Hawai'i remain, and over 75 percent of those remaining are listed as endangered.

It all started when man first came to these isolated islands, and brought and stored water, which added mosquitoes and avian malaria; then came the feral pigs, goats, deer, and sheep, which destroyed much of the Hawaiian forest plants upon which many birds feed. Mongooses are no help either. Nearly one-third of recorded bird extinctions in the past 300 years have occurred here. New birds have been introduced over time, and some native birds are making a comeback—like the nēnē, which probably numbered in the 30s in the 1950s but now number over 3,000 estimated in captivity and in the wild. So man can surely help revive as well as destroy.

So what can you do? And yes, it does matter. Mosquitoes kill more people every year than every other nonhuman animal combined, by far. Perhaps one million deaths annually. Over 400,000 people worldwide die from malaria alone. So heed the call to clean your gutters, remove old tires and water-catching toys in the yard, flush out old ponds and catchment areas. Protect yourself and our avian friends with simple techniques that won't cost you anything but might save us all a lot. Think about it...

September 8, 2016

The Payment Plan Dance

2027. That's when current plans for taxpayer subsidies to the rapid transit are supposed to end. And the legislature has already said it is quite wary about extending that deadline and tax, as it's onerous enough to make taxpayers foot the growing bill for 11 more years. But come on, the Federal Transit Authority announced that they won't pay another penny, at this time. Too many other projects on tap throughout the country right now, as you might expect. And the Feds mandated that this current rail project better make it all the way to Ala Moana Center, as was originally planned and as they were told years ago when they promised funding.

So what to do? Costs aren't suddenly going to slide back from the anticipated $8 billion price tag to $5.8 billion as was originally budgeted unless we make this thing into a luge track. And while it would be easy and cynical to suggest that legislators will simply extend the tax deadline to 3035 or so, the issue must be resolved soon, as the Feds are demanding answers, albeit possibly later than the current end of the year explanation deadline.

The city needs more time to put a payment plan together. "Plan" in this case means more money, for if you build it, they will come—they, as in contractors, engineers, and builders demanding payment. So watch the dancing that goes on now as the city has to get the state to allow us—you and me—to keep paying for the rail beyond 2027, or pay more in taxes before that. It's simple math applied to a very un-simple situation. Pay now or pay later. But pay we will. Think about it...

Anybody wanna bet now on when local taxpayers might stop paying for this runaway train? Check back in three more years, or six years, or nine years...

October 17, 2016

Mongoose on the Loose

A wayward Oʻahu mongoose managed to catch a flight to Kauaʻi last week, though it was captured soon after arrival. Mongooses, natives of India, were introduced here on a few islands over 130 years ago to control rats in our sugar fields. Ah, but rats are nocturnal and mongooses are diurnal, or daytime critters, so it never actually worked out as intended. With no natural predators here, it's a wonder that the wide-eyed buggers haven't found their way to Kauaʻi in droves yet, but my guess is that this lone marauder probably was so taken aback at how bad the Honolulu Airport is, it decided to take a chance to get away from it all. Have you seen the airport lately?

Yellow tape everywhere; escalators not working; lack of air flow in many areas; poorly marked, if any, signage in construction areas; a parking lot with no individual stall markings, making it tough to remember where you parked after a week or so away; bathrooms in disrepair...the list goes on and on. Mongooses are no laughing matter, as Lānaʻi and Kauaʻi are the only local islands where this impish predator has not impacted the local bird and turtle populations. And since the rats simply refuse to play during the day, it looks like the mongoose will continue to have free reign against any natural predators here.

This little fellow was euthanized upon capture, as is the usual protocol, but you have to wonder how many of his or her fellow Rikki-Tikki-Tavis will dare to try and escape through the depressing Honolulu Airport. Maybe they'll simply wait for a ferry to reappear, but at the rate the airport here is being repaired and upgraded, odds are this won't be the last varmint to leave town after seeing the third-world conditions at Honolulu Airport. And this is the first and last place locals and visitors alike see upon arriving in and leaving paradise. Rats! Think about it...

Good news, we're still in the top three nationally in large, domestic airport rankings; bad news, top three as in worst. Big betting game: Which gets finished first, like in 2026, the Hawaiʻi Rapid Transit project or the Honolulu Airport renovations?

Think about it.

October 24, 2016

No Discovery Recovery

When is reality not reality? One instance is when public perception overrides it. The CEO of the Hawai'i Children's Discovery Center, along with others, told us last week in a front page story that it's safe to bring our keiki to the wonderful children's center. But constant news stories, pictures of the homeless still encamped in the area, the sensory disgust of the smell of feces or urine around the center, concerns about parking lot vandalism—these are all tough circumstances to overcome. For many interested parents and grandparents, the idea that you'd be parking your car in a possibly unsafe area and having to deal with unsavory issues is quite enough to keep them from reconsidering a trip down to Kaka'ako.

In an area that should be celebrated for its medical school and children's center, many people still have the sense through their senses— eyes, ears, and noses—that something is afoul and amiss in an area fronting the ocean, which ought to be a cherished place to visit and learn. And until something longer term is developed and in place for the law-abiding but unfortunate, displaced wanderers squatting throughout our towns, it will be a tough marketing effort to make wary parents come back to the Children's Discovery Center in droves.

Revenue there is down 30 percent, according to center CEO/chair Loretta Yajima. No business can afford to have that trend continue. So what will be done beyond what has already been done over the past 18 months to lower the number of people making this area an outdoor home? This is not just a question for a four-block area in Kaka'ako. How many other places are locals avoiding due to perception and reality? Think about it...

Nice to see how far we've come in three years...oh wait. What? Crap... literally, crap!

October 27, 2016

Political Castigating

As political campaigns locally and throughout the country wind up over the next 10 days or so, we hear assumptions about how this must truly be the nastiest presidential campaign ever. On the local front, not so much, as the big races, of which we have far too few, have mostly been devoid of much controversy, enlightenment, accusations, or "oh wow" moments. But for the record, if you look back, all the way back, you'll see just how relatively normal this national election is compared to some pit bull fights in days of yore.

Like back in 1800, when a vice president actually ran against a president. Thomas Jefferson hired a writer and called John Adams a "hermaphroditical character which has neither the force and firmness of a man, nor the gentleness and sensibility of a woman." Challenger Andrew Jackson said of incumbent John Quincy Adams's wife's maid in 1828 that she had been sold as a concubine to the Russian czar. Adams said Jackson had the personality of a dictator and was too uneducated to rule, plus he and his cronies heaped all kinds of insults at Jackson's wife. Ah the good old days. Talk about uncouth campaigns!

Even venerable Abe Lincoln took potshots, referring to his 1860 challenger, Stephen Douglas, as "Little Giant," as Douglas stood five feet four. Lincoln claimed that Douglas was "about five feet nothing in height and about the same in diameter the other way." Douglas called Lincoln a "horrid-looking wretch, sooty, and scoundrelly in aspect," among other things. So relax a bit; the unseemly and venomous diatribe we hear this year is really nothing new. That doesn't make it better; it's just easier than ever to find chatter nowadays on TV via texts, social media, just about anywhere. Good news? It's almost over, and then we can shower and clean up. Think about it...

Can't wait for the 2020 election cycle to kick in with a renewed sense of class by candidates, a focus on the issues, and a sincere willingness to actually represent the voters. Great what we've learned to assuage the masses after almost 250 years?

Think about it

December 8, 2016

War Lessons

75 years ago the United States of America entered into World War II after the attack on Pearl Harbor. So where are we today with our sworn enemies of 1941? Well, our relationship with Japan is solid, and they are a great partner and friend. Germany? Italy? Solid allies of ours in Europe. Edmund Burke was an Anglo-Irish statesman and author over 250 years ago who reportedly said, "Those who don't know history are doomed to repeat it."

So when you look at a world awash in uncertainty and turmoil today, just take a look back at our own history as a nation less than a century ago to see that mortal enemies can not only come to peace, but can actually become great allies. And hopefully it doesn't take the loss of millions of lives to get there. That might seem a bit far-fetched this week as we view with great caution events and leaders in the Middle East, Russia, North Korea, and even northern Africa, but history has shown us that differences about one's place in the world and what's right or wrong can be resolved or mitigated, hopefully without a worldwide conflagration.

Power and control, paranoia and fear, historically based on rigid political, social, economic, and/or religious positions, lead people to make devastating decisions that can impact tens of millions. But the lessons from World War II learned decades after the December 7 attack on our naval base right here in Hawai'i show that somewhere down the road, hopefully without war, people of disparate beliefs, means and ways can get it together for mutual benefit and gain. Naïve? Perhaps, but that's what was said in late 1941, too. Think about it…

Well, the way things are going in Washington, DC, it appears that the ally thing was way overrated for the past 75 years.

Think about it.

December 19, 2016

Tom and a Smile

One of a kind... Perhaps that's an overused sentiment, but it is certainly true about Tom Moffatt. Tom was a friend and business associate of mine for almost 40 years. While I didn't possess his vast knowledge of the music business, he knew that I was a music collector and fanatic, and he would call me from time to time over the years with his inimitable voice and say, "Hey, John, what do you think about so-and-so in concert?"

And then we'd discuss pricing, costs, and relative popularity of the potential concert attraction here and for the Neighbor Islands. By the way, reggae does real well on Hawai'i Island. We did this for over 30 years, and some of my fondest memories in the entertainment world include sitting up in Tom's penthouse perch on Waimanu; actually "penthouse" is too kind a term for the old wooden office he inhabited for years, filled with rock and pop memorabilia and scraps of paper with vital phone numbers. Tom was our conduit to Elvis and Elton, entertaining the masses in his KPOI radio days and then promoting local artists, comedians, international performers, Sesame Street, Shanghai acrobats—you name it, he provided it. And always with a smile.

Over the last 60 years, very few people who lived here did not come across a Tom Moffatt Production at some point. Tom was worldly, local, classy, funny, interesting, and interested. I last visited him a couple months back and gave him a homemade CD compilation of my favorite hits from 1960–62. I hope it gave him a few smiles, for he gave me, and so many others, many, many smiles and concert thrills throughout the years. He will be missed not just for what he did, but for who he was—a class act indeed. Aloha, Tom. Think about it...

Our continued dearth of concerts (for a city the size of Honolulu) reminds us monthly of how much we miss this beloved entrepreneur. And the proposed addition of just 2,200 seats at the Blaisdell won't help.

December 22, 2016

Sweet Sorrow

Commercial sugarcane said aloha mid-month, after a nice run of 146 years. This great state was shaped in so many ways by the dominant agrarian society that consisted mainly of pineapple and sugar, yet we sometimes lose sight of where Hawai'i would be today without these staple crops of yesteryear. Just about everyone who has been here for more than a single generation surely has a story about a relative, neighbor, cohort, or significant other working in the fields, of the influence of this hard work industry on our very day-to-day life.

And while the jobs have disappeared and a local way of life has slowly died off over time, there are other crops and viable options for our fields and for the people who wish to remain in the agricultural area. But Hawai'i was known for its pineapple and sugar for well over 100 years, and immigrants came to Hawai'i from all over southeast Asia, Portugal, and other places to work the fields. Plantation life was more than just a job, and even a malahini like me was enthralled 40 years ago, listening to Goro Arakawa tell me intriguing tales with pictures of Waipahu sugar life as he sat in his store in his vintage palaka shirt.

And while the mongooses never took care of the rats they were assigned to deal with due to lifestyle differences, every other aspect of the laborious field work was handled over the years, until it ultimately became cheaper to get sugar and pineapple from overseas. A way of life, framed by tenacity, scarcity, hard work, and sometimes brutal conditions has come and gone. But in its place is the legacy of generations who can smile when they look back at what brought their kin to these magnificent shores in the first place—someone searching for a new and better life. Sugar and pineapple might be pretty much gone here, but there are many sweet success stories left behind for sure. Think about it...

Sadly, Goro Arakawa passed away in late 2019. He was truly a local treasure.

NC Hey Hey!

If it seems like it took forever, that's because in basketball preparation terms and probable angst, it did take forever. But in its infinite wisdom, the powers that be atop the NCAA and the infractions faction of that austere group, which had apparently jumped the gun when it did a mea culpa publicly about UH sanctions four months ago before checking with the top dogs, have finally decided to let the kids play. Other sanctions were also shaved back, included probationary window for the basketball squad and its scholarship availabilities.

The change was made, according to the NCAA, because the NCAA changed the penalty structure against UH from a Level II Aggravated case to a Level II Standard case. The NCAA stated last Friday that "...the current penalty structure was found to be more lenient due to the change in case classification. Therefore the panel reduced the scholarship penalty and probation and eliminated the postseason ban."

That wording almost makes the NCAA look like angels who have now suddenly deemed UH to be somewhat OK, when in fact, the NCAA went too far in the first place in its sanctions, but at least it now has righted the wrongs, perhaps realizing that the so-called adults who ran the men's basketball program a couple of years back arrogantly overstepped their bounds, and then supposedly lied about it when officially questioned. Now, let's play ball in the Big West tourney; good on these kids who came together from afar with few expectations this season and have been competitive week in and week out in 2017. Go 'Bows! Think about it...

The NCAA (No Clue At All) is trembling at the issues it deflects, excuses, ignores, or gets trampled over by the too-powerful conferences and universities which it ostensibly serves.

Un-loha

I've heard whispers, hints, and allegations over the years, but I really didn't perceive it deeply. Now I'm beginning to wonder. Is some of the magic of "aloha" disappearing here? I see it in traffic, where everyone would wave out the window or with their right hand when you let them into your lane. Now, not so much. In a.m. or p.m. traffic, everyone's in a rush and trying to wedge into the lane or make the last-second move into the right lane to get off as opposed to properly planning 15 seconds earlier; like it's their divine right to move right. And the net gain in this calculated or clueless move—nada, zip, nothing, less than five seconds. And not even a friendly mahalo wave or a shaka? Lighten up, Jimmy Johnson, you'll get there.

Even TheBus system has taken the concept of thanks away from humans, as now we see an electronic shaka sign often appear atop the right rear of the bus when you let a bus driver in. I guess the left hand needs to remain on the wheel these days. And that moron who cuts me off to zip by usually ends up waiting at the same red light that I do. I consider that a small victory for humanity. Impatience is one thing; I'm quite familiar with that. But rudeness and lack of aloha—that's beneath us, isn't it?

You see it in parking lots when you let people in ahead of you. No wave, just a subtle sense of entitlement. You see it at retailers when Christmas shopping. "Merry Christmas," but I'll remove an appendage of yours if you grab that last Shimmer & Shine Doll that my daughter has to have. Happy holidays, indeed. We need to keep perspective, even when the walls seem to be closing in. Chill, everybody. Let rudeness rule in Washington, DC; New York City; or Chicago. We're better than that here, aren't we? Well, except for the people who need a "Defend Hawaii" sticker on their car juxtaposed with a "Live Aloha" one! Think about it...

July 17, 2017

Breaking New Ground

The fact that groundbreaking on a project to build new homes for the homeless took place near Sand Island last week is groundbreaking unto itself. That a public–private concoction could conceive of and actually begin work on such a project without far too many committees, studies, and meetings over the past year is extraordinary, and a testament to the skill, passion, and commitment of local businessman Duane Kurisu and others.

While far too many projects and ideas locally get discussed, tossed around, and often times ignored, this project is now under way and should see the first families moving in before year end. Astounding! All of the parties involved, both public and private, had to come together to make this dream become a reality in record time. And the plan here is to provide the people in need with a community, not just basic living quarters. Another local business guru has even offered jobs in the nearby area for those committed to working, so that they can possibly walk to work.

And as excitement and buildings grow, the obvious question is: What's next and where's next? For if this project can work, flourish, and lead as an example, perhaps a bigger dent can be made in the homeless situation throughout our state when other like-minded business executives work with the system, or help to change it, to make a big difference in many people's lives. After all, isn't that one of the reasons we are all here in the first place— to make a difference? Kudos to Kurisu! Think about it...

It's working. It's not a theory, a plan, a study; it's working, it's growing. Where's the next one going to be located? Mini units are now up in Waipahu, as we inch along in resolving homelessness.

July 20, 2017

Texting Lawbreakers

The city council approved a bill last week that makes it a crime for people to look at their phones or other electronic device while walking across the street. Fines will be issued for guilty parties who are caught. The mayor is looking closely at the bill's details. Not a day goes by where you don't see people busy looking at their Angry Birds, Candy Crush, or vital update on Justin Bieber while walking in an intersection, usually oblivious to traffic. Add to that the ignorati texting as they cruise through the intersection or make a right turn on red, and well...the possibility for a sad news story is out there every day.

OK, but what do we do about the people just as clueless who talk on the phone while walking on the streets? That habit did not get included in the bill. And what about people who gab with friends in the intersection or pick at their french fry bags with heads down while walking? Those social norms are apparently still appropriate in the early 21st century here in Honolulu.

Remember way back when people used to walk and actually look at the sites around them? Or watch a movie and actually talk to each other afterwards before checking their phones? Ah yes, that was a simpler, more pastoral time—like, five years ago. 4.2 billion people text nowadays. 81 percent of Americans text every day. 97 percent of American adults text weekly. 95 percent of texts will be read within three minutes of being sent. Average response time is 90 seconds. Heck, some couples don't respond that quickly when their significant other is sitting in the same room. Well, maybe this new texting/walking law will change some of these ridiculous and addictive behaviors in Hawai'i. Hey, thumb guru. Heads up and I mean heads up, HPD is watching you. Think about it...

If a driver is texting and plows through a crosswalk and hits a pedestrian texting while walking, does anyone hear it?

Think about it

Starstruck

The eclipse last week was great, though we didn't get to see much of it here due to angles and all. Work productivity dropped or stopped all across the country as people looked, but not too closely we hope, at this rare phenomenon. Space exploration is really cool. We have a chance, though it might be slipping away as the clock ticks, to be the home of an amazing telescope amid obvious controversy. We hear from time to time about possible exoplanets or systems way out there that might, just might, contain water or Earth-like atmospheres. One of these orbs is apparently only 22 light-years, or 132 trillion miles, away, which means at current spacecraft speeds, it would take about 100,000 years or so to get there—just to see if it's habitable.

Sometimes space talk and some dreams seem rather silly. Yes, exploration is great; it's gotten us to where we are today as a species. But we've got enough issues on Earth that really smart people who look up could probably help a great deal with if they would just look down—or under—the earth's surface or the oceans. No, I'm not a killjoy, and I did enjoy at least the first series of Star Wars movies, but sometimes the vague notion that there might be something or someone out there seems to override the fact that we could sure use more help from smart minds and scientific money to resolve some issues right here at home, on planet Earth.

We should always dream big and make our goal to reach for the stars in many endeavors, but we also need to work pragmatically, intensively, and relentlessly to explore the best means of discovery right here in our own solar system and on our current planet to ensure that we can thrive for the next millennium or two. Like Dr. Spock said, "Live long and prosper." Think about it...

People are malnourished or dehydrated throughout the world, and we're supposed to get excited about an orb that might have water on it 100 million miles away? Let's focus on our ocean floors, rain forests, and deserts; let's make a difference on this orb in this millennium.

August 31, 2017

Women Work

Website WalletHub told us last week that Hawai'i ranks number one of all the states in the country when it comes to "women's equality." Hawai'i ranked number one in "education and health" and "smallest income gap," number eight in "political empowerment," and number four in "workplace environment" among the 15 key indicators used to define gender equality. The study looked at the number of male and female executives, unemployment rates, and other measurable areas in making its analysis. Nevada ranked number two, followed by Illinois and Minnesota, so there's no geographical slant in this tabulation. Texas, Virginia, and Utah ranked at the bottom of the equality survey.

Internationally, the US ranks only 45th out of 144 ranked countries in gender equality. While WalletHub says that women in this country make up 49 percent of the college-educated labor force, only six percent are CEOS and just 25 percent hold executive or senior management positions nationwide. And while there are numerous theories to explain this disparity, the reality is we've still got a long way to go. And the gaps are much worse for minorities, male or female. Glass ceiling? Not so bad here, but in other places the ceiling appears to be concrete.

Over the past 60 years, 49 democracies worldwide have elected at least one woman to lead, including 15 as of today. That list includes Germany, Bangladesh, Estonia, South Korea, India, Brazil, Iceland, Israel, Pakistan, Turkey, and Sri Lanka. In almost 250 years, the US hasn't managed to elect a woman to its top spot. In Hawai'i, we've seen minorities and women lead us, and they've done it quite well. The gender gap in many places in this country is growing. I know it's just a website and some data, but this is one glowing title—number one in gender equality—that Hawai'i should be proud of and continue to set the national trend. Think about it...

As it should be, forevermore. You go, girl!

The Storm That May Come

Hurricanes recently generated wind damage plus massive rain and ocean flooding in Texas and then in Florida, wildfires rage today in California, and in the northwest—disasters with huge consequences immediately and for months and possibly years ahead. While damage is being assessed and people try to resume some sense of normalcy in their lives amid the tragedy and its aftereffects, you hope that other areas prone to similar circumstances and the government entities entrusted therein will learn valuable lessons that can be learned from these events to help mitigate the trauma and damage elsewhere for the next time that nature erupts.

The question of a strong hurricane hitting our islands at some level is really a question of when, not if. We have been fortunate of late as advancing hurricanes have skirted our shores, drifted north or south or broken up before causing cataclysmic damage. Hurricane Iniki arrived in mid-September of 1992; it killed six people, left almost 1,000 injured and caused over $1.8 billion in damages (that's over $3 billion in 2017 dollars) as it slammed into Kaua'i after first threatening our tourist and economic hub on the south shores of O'ahu.

How much better prepared are we now then we were 25 years ago? How much safer or stronger is our infrastructure? How much better are vital communication standards today in case of widespread power outages? How fast can relief come our way with no adjacent states to help provide power, blankets, or water? How viable are contingency plans? How have new buildings, roads, and infrastructure affected possible flood zones and the threat of seawater surge over the past quarter century? These are just a few of the questions that hopefully have been addressed and answered by the powers that be locally as we thrive in our tropical paradise—somewhat defenseless vs. the perhaps inevitable wrath of Mother Nature. Think about it...

It would be great to have the answers to these questions handled with certainty and confidence today.

September 21, 2017

Comfortably Numb

Numb. That's what time and redundancy can do to the human mind. And that's what a lot of people feel right now as it relates to the rail issue. Here are just some of the recent headlines: "Rail officials start over on selecting builder for last stretch," "Ige signs bill giving state added control over rail," "Rail vote could cost House leader her post," "Council finalizes extension of GET surcharge to cover rail shortfall," "Rail bailout forever weds State to project."

When it rains, it pours, and the rapid transit dream, which began with much hype and hope, now seems to be approaching a nightmare state, like the sinkhole discovered by Ala Moana Regional Park last week—a treacherous hole that needs to be fixed. We keep filling rail project holes with money, topped off with leadership changes, new dances with the Feds, a decision to not look back and learn from past mistakes—the list goes on and on. And all this for a choo choo that is still at least eight years away from being fully ready.

I am not a rail fatalist. But I have grown skeptical of promises and reassurances after seeing what we've all witness unfold thus far, and that's knowing we've got the biggest and most convoluted construction segments yet to come as the project hits the congested corridors of Kalihi, downtown, and Kaka'ako. Over $10 billion from an original expectation of less than $6 billion for this train? Well, some are saying it could actually reach $13 billion. Numb is bad, but dumb is worse. Let's make sure smart people and smart answers come forward as we try to keep rail on the tracks. Think about it.

And if you felt numb over two years ago, I can only imagine how you feel…er, hello. Um…is anybody listening?

Think about it

October 23, 2017

Hangar's On

Hawaiian Airlines fixed some problems in a cargo and maintenance hangar at Honolulu's airport, now officially called the Daniel K. Inouye International Airport, though one has to wonder what our late esteemed senator would say about his name being attached to the facility if he saw the ever-increasing, shoddy conditions prevalent in far too many places of our main airport. Anyway, Hawaiian Air fixed the problems that it didn't create in this hangar, and stated recently that there were over 3,500 issues found on the project, ranging from cracked concrete before anyone even drove over the area, ramps that were poorly designed, walls with dysfunctional electricity setups, etc. Yes, over 3,500 issues that cropped up or were present.

Hawaiian Air CEO Mark Dunkerley is now calling upon the state to find out what went wrong, why it went wrong, and why there were so many delays and subcontractor defections throughout this project, which was obviously important enough for Hawaiian Air to come in and complete in less than a year...correctly. Lawsuits are in place, with more to follow, no doubt, as this project was designed to cost $85 million but will end up costing about $120 million, according to published reports. And this one isn't even a rapid transit snafu!

As bad conditions are at this airport which everyone sees when coming to or leaving Oʻahu, the delays in this single project have had a domino effect in delaying the removal and movement of the commuter terminal as well as many other projects. So, will we see a clear answer as to what went wrong and who was accountable on this seven-year project, let alone over 3,500 answers? If history is our guide, don't bet on it. It's just how business is done, or not done, far too often in Hawaiʻi. Ho hum...pass the bread, please. Think about it...

Perhaps it should be called "In No Way" Airport instead of "Inouye" to reflect the reality.

October 26, 2017

Angry 'Burbs

Hawai'i drivers tend to be courteous and generally accepting of our bad roads and worsening traffic, right? We don't honk, we wave people through intersections; you know the routine. Yet a recent study from Insurance Quotes suggests that Hawai'i has the angriest drivers in the nation, the most road rage of any state. The data came from over 65,000 Instagram posts between mid-2013 and August of 2016. Fridays had the most posts, and August was the angriest month of the year. More traffic heading into weekends and summertime blues.

According to this latest survey, Hawai'i at number one in anger had 67 percent more #RoadRage posts than the second angriest state—California, another state known for lots of cars and lots of traffic all of the time. Heck, years ago, road rage meant shootings in Cali. Road rage postings rise throughout the day nationally, perhaps indicating that drivers simply get more fed up with their lives, let alone driving, as the day wears on, and many feel the need to vent, probably while driving. How unsafe and one more reason to avoid social platforms more often. The survey blames our road rage on incessant traffic and also suggests that the driving and sometimes clueless tourists might be ratcheting up our road rage. Yes, some of those street names are tough to fathom for first-time visitors going 12 miles per hour. And bikers with maps in their hands doesn't help our auto weaving.

New York ranked number three in road rage. The home of honking when you're 12th in line and the light turns green. You really expect me to believe that Hawai'i residents and visitors are angrier and ruder while driving than those in New York? Maybe the flaw here is that many of us simply don't use Instagram, ever! Maybe our real anger nowadays is about the plethora of surveys purported to be factual, which now show up far too often about far too many subjects with far too many variables. Maybe more people should stop providing us with 24-hour instantaneous answers on things, and spend more time simply reflecting. You know, think about it...

Think about it...

November 6, 2017

Oh Boy, Opioid

Staggering...the numbers are simply staggering. We hear repeatedly nowadays about the dangers of opioid use and abuse in America. Years ago, that normally meant heroin, methamphetamine, or cocaine addiction. But not anymore. The growing culprit today is not only legal, it's very often prescribed. Check out these statistics from various sources: 91 percent of poison deaths in Hawai'i over a five-year span came from illegal or prescribed drugs. Hawai'i sees a drug overdose death almost once every two days— that's 15 people monthly and that's actually four percent better our overdose numbers from two years ago.

80 percent of heroin users started by misusing prescription drugs. Five years ago, 260 million prescriptions were written in this country for pain-killing opioids—that's enough to supply one bottle to every single adult in America. The US is home to a little less than five percent of the world's population, yet we are responsible for 80 percent of the world's opioid use, legal and illegal. I always thought we were the tough, cowboy kinda nation, but apparently, we experience more pain than any other nation in the world... by far.

The lobbying effort of the drug makers is profound, as they've spent almost $900 million in campaign contributions and lobbying efforts since 2016, according to the Honolulu Star-Advertiser. And Hawai'i is not immune to this, though lobbying here is perceived to be minimal relative to other places. America and Hawai'i need to get a grip on pain—from the doctors to Big Pharma to the lawmakers. Suffering pain is horrible, but the solution doesn't have to be addiction or death. At least not in the rest of the world. Think about it...

Think about it.

December 7, 2017

Guns and Ganja

The Hawaiʻi Police Department just reviewed its recently announced policy that anyone who is legally using cannabis (or marijuana) on Oʻahu must turn in his or her firearms and ammunition within 30 days of receiving a letter from HPD. 30 legal marijuana users got the letters, and federal law dictates that an "unlawful user" of a controlled substance, a class which marijuana finds itself in, may not possess firearms. According to federal law, marijuana is a Schedule I controlled substance, like heroin, and it simply cannot be used legally. The DEA claims that marijuana has not been proven to be safe and effective by the Food & Drug Administration, and thus it refuses to budge on the Schedule I profiling of marijuana...after 47 years of complaints.

While HPD won't confiscate guns from medical marijuana users, it will deny new permits to those with a medical marijuana card. This once again points out problems associated with the fact that more and more states now allow the use of marijuana either for medical patients or recreationally for anyone over the age of 21 with a belly button. It is all very confusing how a substance that's banned nationally can be OK'ed locally, kind of. Then there's the whole bank issue, as in where do dispensaries park their money, since banks cannot accept drug money.

One can only hope that as more states see the multicolored light and start easing the restrictions on marijuana, that the federal government better defines its plans. Alcohol drinkers aren't asked to turn in their weapons, yet the list of crimes committed while using alcohol is well known, including robbery, aggravated assault, sexual assault, child abuse, and homicide. 40 percent of convicted murderers used alcohol before or during their crimes. Everyone needs a clearer definition of the dos and don'ts related to marijuana use, recreationally or for medicinal purposes. The local policy related to firearms ownership and medical marijuana usage is really just one piece of a much bigger puzzle that needs to become a lot less hazy in the coming years. Think about it...

Good news. Our reluctant legislature can now pick up the phone and see how it's going in Colorado, Oregon, California, Washington, Maine, Vermont...

Think about it

163

December 14, 2017

A Taxing Situation

What part of the concept "independent consultant" is so difficult to comprehend? The entity hired to oversee the overhaul of the antiquated, failing state computer system had fingers in its pie far too often, it seems from people who should and do know better. The only time I've heard the word "meddle" used in a good way is when referencing the album Meddle by Pink Floyd, and that was released 46 years ago!

We consistently show an apparent leadership void at so many major moments in time here on issues like the TMT, homelessness, affordable housing, the Waikīkī natatorium, the Stairway to Heaven, etc. We have the uncanny ability to meddle, to call for further studies, to minimize needed change by just doing the same old, same old. We elect the same officials over and over with minimal quality opposition, I get it, yet wonder why things don't get resolved, which would obviously involve some bruised feelings and wounded egos. It's because far too often we would rather get along and go along than do the right thing or the necessary thing.

Avoid conflict, competition, situations of unease, responsibility, and blame. No make A. I get it, to some degree. Who wants to be the fall guy or the scapegoat? And yes, drama sucks, except when it's in our music or on our TV, digital, and movie screens. Drama is bad for your physical and mental health. Avoid it whenever possible. But resolution and admitting wrongs is part of the deal, especially for people in high places, like elected and appointed officials. The state tax director quit last week. Is that the end of this meddling saga? No one is apparently at fault far too often in far too many situations locally. It's the system, and hey, I just work here. I'll smile regularly, put in my time, get my pension and lifelong medical coverage, and someone else can fix things later. Please, just leave me alone. Think about it...

Or as we call it in Hawai'i—Tuesday (or Monday, or Friday).

Memorable Mentors

January is National Mentoring Month, which, according to a mentoring website, is meant to provide an annual, high-profile campaign to draw attention to the need for more volunteer mentors to help America's young people achieve their full potential. Locally, we have a great deal of respect for our elders, our kūpuna, and we depend on so many of them to provide insight and lessons along the way.

Whether it be at work, at home, on sports teams, in organizations or just informally, working with a mentor can provide lifelong lessons and insights to anyone who cares to pay attention. People from Maya Angelou, President Obama, Clint Eastwood, Senator John McCain, Quincy Jones, Cal Ripken Jr., Usher, and other notable people of accomplishment have shown their support for mentoring to ensure that the next generations have some appropriate guidelines to help them along the way as they become our leaders of tomorrow.

There is plenty of information online for those of you who wish to more formally mentor locally. Mentorship locally is a great way for people to pass along a lifetime of lessons learned, how to achieve goals both personal and professional, overcoming adversity, working alongside others with disparate viewpoints, showing integrity and all of the other traits that make people we all know such worthy mentors. We have so many wonderful role models in our midst in Hawai'i. Become one, align with one, or seek one out if you're on your way up. Positive outcomes for our keiki through local mentors is real and possible every day here. Think about it.

A perfect way to give back for those who are recently retired and have time to spare and time to share...

Basic Economics

Only 20 states in this country mandate that each and every high school graduate has some basic sense of personal finance and economics. And that makes no sense. While learning trigonometry about cosines is great, knowing what it means to cosign a bank document is surely of greater importance later in life. And while it's important to understand the concept of a right angle, it's more important to understand the pragmatic nature of what angle to take when approaching credit card debt, student loans, and a mortgage that might end up oppressing you for years. 70 percent of adults recently scored a C or worse on a nationwide economics exam.

According to the National Council for Economic Education, 25 percent of millennials spend more than they earn; 67 percent of Generation Y has less than 90 days of emergency funds available to them. 97 percent of adults think economics should be taught in school. 93 percent of students agree. We can augment that necessary change here in Hawai'i by working with the Department of Education to ensure that every child graduates high school with at least the basics to help them move toward a financially stable life. Economic ignorance often leads to lower financial opportunities and weaker outcomes. Maybe it needs to be a middle school class to catch all kids as some drop out in high school. Maybe freshman year is the ideal time. We just need to figure out how to tweak existing school schedules and work in at least a month or so of solid, but basic, vital economic education.

We need teachers trained and rewarded at every high school or middle school throughout the state as we need to bring personal finance and a basic set of money skills to our keiki before they hit the real world. There is no doubt, none, that financial literacy pays dividends. We talk about teaching physical and mental health, well it's time for pushing financial health in our schools. Let's work together with the DOE and state legislators this session to get a game plan going to enact this concept already working in 20 states. Let's make sure that future generations here stay ahead of the game and don't fall into a financial pit due to ignorance. Reading, 'riting, and 'rithmetic are great, but not more so than the real-world value of economic knowledge. Think about it...

February 5, 2018

Housing and Fences and You

A couple of local government building suggestions highlighted recently have caught my attention: the Hawai'i Public Housing Authority is working with other entities on plans to build some affordable housing along the transit line in Pearl Highlands, near Aloha Stadium, and in Kalihi. Mores sites will hopefully be identified soon and then development plans can begin. Let's hope that red tape is avoided, as multiple agencies will be involved; let's make sure the unit costs are truly affordable for regular wage earners locally; and let's get these edifices built before the complete rail system is fully operational—because that's at least eight years away.

As hopeful and positive as the transit-oriented development projects are sounding, there is another story about a ridiculous estimate for a fence to be built around the Hawaii State Hospital, which would cost between $17 and $24 million. Yes, that's right, for a fence. You could probably enhance internal security at the state facility for far less than $20 million or so for an outdoor fence, a fence topped with barbed wire. And of course, if people can walk out the front door unattended to, a fence isn't going to be the best answer at the Kāne'ohe facility. Perhaps the fence is a Gucci or Versace design, and thus the price tag suggested is realistic and fair.

We see some positive signs for housing and a questionable suggestion for a costly fence around a facility that has far bigger internal pukas than this fence would solve. Bills are rushing through the legislature and some will impact you, no doubt. Are you paying attention and responding? Are you calling or emailing or showing up to testify? Or will you simply prefer to gripe when all is said and done come early May? Think about it...

"Affordable housing" is an overused, undefined term that means different things to different people. One thing it does mean is talking ad nauseum about the issue without any major gains being made. More people move away, or simply don't come home after college on the mainland, because there are just too few "affordable" units to rent or buy.

Local Media Are Emergency Conduits

Thousands of bills are brought forth in our annual legislative session, of which about one percent will actually get passed. One of the major areas of concern in 2018 is emergency preparedness and safety, and we all know why. Thus I found it interesting upon looking at this 119-page document, the State of Hawaii Emergency Operations Plan, from May of 2017, that there is just one half of one page in here dedicated to actual communications with the general public, beyond the EAS System—which broadcasters don't control.

There's plenty in this plan addressing how officials will take care of talking to one another in the event of a devastating hurricane, earthquake, tsunami, etc., but when it comes to including the primary conduits to the general public and our visitors—that would be the local broadcast community of over 100 television and radio stations—this lengthy tome spends scant time making sure that these entities have all of the modern tools and plans in place from officials to ensure that we can alert you and your loved ones. Why? Because no one asked us, that's why. This state plan is an attempt to organize and coordinate emergency management activities to save lives, protect people and property, but not much thought was given to ensure that local media were included and queried on how to make sure that we can help to get important information out to everyone.

While broadcasters are federally regulated, we are always happy to work, when contacted, with state and county officials—especially in times of need, or possible need. But if the power is out, if phones don't work or are clogged, if our closed captioners' computers aren't able to provide that vital service? Do we have two-way communication devices in place for official updates? My plea today is to make sure that our legislators reach out to include the broadcast community and other conduits to the public when making laws and proposing emergency system upgrades, for local TV and radio are the first life lines for Hawai'i's people in times of need. More than just an EAS alert, we provide succinct data and vital details, when we know. And yes, we do it quicker, accurately and in depth when feasible, and much better than Twitter or Facebook. Think about it…

Housing History

The governor wrote, "I approved the State Housing Functional Plan. This plan is based on joint public and private efforts to finance, build, and maintain an adequate supply of affordable housing for Hawai'i's people. This is not a goal that will be easily or quickly attained." He also wrote that "…our plan has its shortcomings. It does not address to a sufficient degree those individuals or families who can least afford safe, decent shelter."

Strong, definitive words and an action plan. The trouble is that this foreword to an addendum to the State Housing Functional Plan was written by Governor John Waihee, and the year was 1990. The report cites an estimation of 7,000 to 9,400 homeless people throughout Hawai'i on any given day. And that was 28 years ago. A 2016 report here estimated that we had 7,900 homeless people. So the number of homeless has perhaps not changed drastically in the past 28 years, but those in need are no longer hanging just under the freeways off of Nimitz Highway or communing on leeward coast beaches. They are in Kaka'ako by the UH Medical School, they're on viaducts near downtown, they're hovering around Waikīkī, they're on the windward side.

So where are the mental health volunteers and real public–private partnerships in the year 2018 to provide hope and truly affordable housing? How far have we come as living costs have shot up in 28 years but disposable income has not kept pace for far too many here? A $750,000 dwelling unit is simply not "affordable." Where are the $300,000 units created through great incentives and government–private partnerships? We need 10 more Kahauiki Villages. It seems like we're always hearing the same thing when it comes to housing: stay tuned. As The Who succinctly said some 47 years ago, "Meet the new boss, same as the old boss!" Think about it…

Sadly, this editorial could be repeated every three months, it seems, until some innovative plans and real actions are taken on truly affordable housing, economic alternatives, homelessness, public–private partnerships, and more professional volunteerism.

February 22, 2018

Unicameral Logic

A local media friend of mine was having a conversation with a state legislator about a proposed bill being pushed through a committee the said legislator served on that would affect the local broadcasting community and some of its local responsibilities. My friend questioned why such a bill was written without any input from the federally regulated broadcasters. The legislator responded by saying, "Oh, and I suppose that if we put forth a bill affecting the elderly we would have to check in with AARP first?!" Well, yeah, that might be a good entity to check in with, just to run it by a stakeholder or two or 200,000.

In the rush to hustle through our local and perhaps too brief legislative session, sometimes bills come up that will affect constituents who aren't even involved in crafting or commenting on said bills until they reach the floor. Time and effort could be saved by discussing potential edicts months in advance. Right now, only 10 percent of crafted bills make it all the way through here each year. Voters must be shown that their legislators care, so a bundle of bills is sent forward, only to die in a committee or when crossing over to the House or Senate or when evaluated.

Perhaps a single legislative body that works full-time could help end this incessant rush to jam things through in short order every January and February. A unicameral—one legislative body—system has been in place in Nebraska for over 80 years, and it is legally nonpartisan. With one full-time legislative body, you could pay higher salaries, hire more assistants, and probably get more work done with forethought and input more regularly. Certainly it's worth talking about in a small state like ours. The odds? OK, good talk. Thanks. Think about it...

A full-time, highly accountable, unicameral legislative body? Fewer ethical concerns, cost savings, quicker actions taken, less confusion among voters. It's surely worth exploring here based on what we see (and don't see) every year.

Year of the Hawaiian

It wasn't a front-page story, there were no fireworks to kick it off, so that might tell you something about its overall value or relevance, unfortunately, but the governor proclaimed 2018 as the Year of the Hawaiian via a Senate resolution on February 16. I hope this celebration or acknowledgment brings with it a proactive effort to deal with some of the issues confronting our hosts in the year 2018 and beyond. After all, in my mind, last year and next year will also be the years of the Hawaiian, as were the past couple of hundred years here.

For it is truly the love for the culture and the initial settlers here that makes the concept of Hawaiian and Hawai'i so special. It is a culture steeped in stories of integrity, faith, connectivity, and respect for the land, ocean, and humanity, which continues on proudly today with so many challenges, yet also so much opportunity to teach not only those who live here, but tens of millions of others who either visit or understand, even at a surface level, that there really is something special about the concept of being and living Hawaiian.

Let's hope that in this Year of the Hawaiian, powers that be deal with cultural issues left unresolved high on a Big Island mountaintop or in the quest for real answers on what is sovereignty. Let's make sure that more focus is given and more answers are found related to housing, education, and health issues, which disproportionately affect keiki o ka 'āina. Yes, if this really is to be the Year of the Hawaiian, then let's see real action springing forth from this resolve.

If we're going to recognize and commit to the Hawaiian community in 2018 through a proclamation, then let's make sure we continue to do so in 2019 and beyond, to remind all people living here amid this rich culture and tradition that the concept and reality of being Hawaiian is central to our daily, local lives and is the benchmark for how we act toward all. This should never be taken for granted in a profound place that so many of us happily call home. Reinforcing, fixing, taking responsibility to augment change—that would really be nice to see in the Year of the Hawaiian. Think about it...

Actually, 2019 might be looked back on someday as the Year of the Hawaiian, with civil activism for many causes statewide.

Wai'anae and Mars

We truly are a planet of mixed metaphors and strange realities. On the one hand, I got an email from a viewer who said her nephew lives in a truck in the Waianae Boat Harbor. She said he and countless others living in cars at the harbor and nearby were never included in the actual count of how many people live there. So who knows what the real numbers are? We just know that there are once again far too many people with far too few solutions.

And then we have the Mars simulation mission, which has been put on hold due to a medical condition of one of the crew members. The NASA-funded mission to try to recreate what it might be like on a planet with little oxygen and travel plans years away has been put on hold 8,200 feet above sea level, while we can't figure out how to deal with sewage and trash dumping and perhaps can't even count how many people are really affected.

We have put on hold a $1 million project to study human interaction in a dome on a mountain simulating, maybe, a less-than-friendly orb 34 million miles away of which we have incomplete data, yet we can't figure out how to do a better job getting reasonable housing or even the water bill paid for earth-bound inhabitants at sea level in Wai'anae, let alone under the highways and near the medical school. Maybe we should can the Mars plan and let the homeless use the domes right here on sea level earth? Space travel? This one's just spacy? Think about it...

Think about it

March 5, 2018

Accountability Lapse

All kinds of state agencies have come under fire lately for alleged misappropriation of funds or some form of fiduciary negligence. State salary overpayments; issues at HTA, OHA, HART...pick an acronym—it's probably being questioned. Some of these instances will surely be explained once the details and circumstances can be better understood, but there is obviously a clear cry for more accountability and transparency. Some may argue that the complaints may be politically motivated, or that the questions asked are really just business as usual.

Except that business as usual in the private sector has many checks and balances along the way, including job security. As in, if you don't keep your financial house in order or make ends meet, you oftentimes lose your job—and you know that. But it's not so easy on the public side of things. There are all kinds of protection in place, ways to deflect accountability all over the place. The bucks stop here, no, here, no, here.

One of the reasons things sometime take so long in officialdom is that many people simply don't want to rock the boat, put themselves on the line, augment change or suggest things that might entail more work or a change in how work is done. That leads to stasis, a period of inactivity. Sometimes that inactivity lasts for years. Which is often why things don't change, don't get resolved, and don't get done when it comes to government projects, initiatives, and internal evolution. As Bruce Hornsby once sang, "That's just the way it is…" Think about it…

 **Think** about it.

March 26, 2018

Repo Republicans

Bravery or politically savvy? That's the question some are asking after last week's announcement that biennial political candidate Charles Djou has become the latest local defector from the Republican Party. This follows on the heels of disillusion and disownment from city council member Kymberly Pine, which followed the March 2017 defection of state House Republican leader Beth Fukumoto. While each politico left for somewhat different reasons, the underlying theme was a perceived lack of party tolerance, barbed commentary from the right, and/or a general lack of respect for the current president.

Whatever the reasons, the sardonic slogan "…will the last one out please turn off the lights," seems to be close to becoming a Republican reality here. Zero state senators out of 25, just five House reps out of 51, and now a loss in the city council, a group which shifts leadership and committee chairs about as often as the sun rises. Whatever your leanings, the Republican representation fallout doesn't bode well for vital legislative checks and balances, alternative points of view, compromising when valid, and all of those other things a good two-party system is supposed to ensure for the general populace in a democracy.

Whether or not you want to argue that fiscally conservative or deeply religious Democrats here are really akamai Republicans dressed in blue clothing for convenience sake, the mere fact that the elected or the possibly electable group of Republicans who work in Hawai'i continues to dwindle as more established members say aloha has got to make you wonder what's up with the party system. Elected Democrats often can't get along in the legislative branch and thus shift chairs and allegiances frequently. We had a near purge in the state House, we have multiple Democratic challengers opposing our incumbent governor come August, and on the other side of the political party spectrum, we now hear nary a word, as far too many have left for what they feel isn't right, or even centrist. Think about it…

A two-party system often feels confining and frustrating, but a one-party system is simply wrong, even if it's your own party. Some may even be singing, "It's my party and I'll cry if I want to." (Kudos to Lesley Gore, 1963.)

April 12, 2018

Chicken Spin

You probably heard about the feral chicken problem that has popped up once again in various places throughout Oʻahu. It is also an obvious issue on Neighbor Islands. After the last program a couple of years ago resulted in a city of Honolulu cost that came out to $108 per chicken caught, that program was fricasseed. Now the city says it will try to work with the state on how best to handle the growing and clucking problem.

One major area of concern is that the chickens don't just stand there, awaiting capture. They choose their flight over fight response, and once they head to private property, well, now you've got liability concerns and other issues. Yes, now you do know why the chicken crossed the road—to avoid capture on public property. One solution suggested using chicken infertility drugs, but that might become a religious issue, so forget it. Another idea was to use youngsters to collect chickens for a reward—but that's probably slave labor, and wait until the kids find out where the chickens (or chicks) end up. Now you've got post-traumatic stress counseling issues, so forget it.

This is not a joke. We need this noisy nuisance to be negated. We need to ferret out these fertile, feral fowl. We have to have a change in official philosophy, a real chicken shift. Heck, even the top restaurants in town don't charge $108 per chicken. Let's hope that the city and state can come up with a plan to mitigate the marauding miscreants, and let's hope that we can soon say that the answer was as easy as duck soup, whatever that means. Think about it…

April 23, 2018

Kaua'i Concerns

The question now for Kaua'i's north shore and other areas there is: What's next? Where will the money come from to better situate roadways and drainage systems before the next big storm? How will engineers design systems to better prepare for overflowing rivers—whether through building berms or providing stronger and more consistent egress for drainage. And how quickly can design, funding, and building be implemented?

The incredible outreach of neighbors and others to provide food, clothing, water, and shelter immediately after the deluge on Kaua'i this month shows what a great and connected community there is on the Garden Island. It's not just the topography on our westernmost island that's so lush and rich, it's the quality of the people themselves; giving and sharing while facing adversity with ingenuity and through immediate action. But now it's time for officials to make sure quickly that shelters do not become islands themselves, that vehicular access is more readily available through redesign and perhaps redirection of some waterways.

Kaua'i has felt the brunt of some of our worst storms over the past 40 years and bounced back with a resiliency that is to be admired. But Kaua'i should not be left alone like some poor, third-world entity looking for help. Like all of our at-risk islands, Kaua'i needs planning and funding now, today, from Līhu'e to Hanalei and beyond, to help ensure that while nature works on its own schedule, people in charge must quickly provide the best answers and plans to minimize damage and trauma via intelligence, local and federal funding, and decisive action. Think about it…

And plans have since been put in place, limiting the number of visitors on a daily basis.

May 3, 2018
No Fun Raising

Among the many reasons that potential local voters give for not showing up or sending in a ballot is the lack of competition, we have a one-party system here, things don't seem to change much, including the candidates, etc., etc. Well, sure, the system needs some fine-tuning, locally and nationally. But one thing here that can be adjusted is the obvious conflict of interest that takes place year after year when part-time legislators vote on things that obviously impact, directly or indirectly, their other jobs and raise campaign funds while in session.

It's not enough to have an ethics base that suggests lawmakers recuse themselves, it's the tie-ins to spouses and their jobs, relatives, etc. And the fact that most savvy legislators know how best to play the system, and know that about 70 percent of eligible residents over the age of 18 don't choose to vote here anyway and well, the decision appears easy. So let's make it uneasy. Let's force more complete disclosure about influences and outside jobs before the legislature meets annually, or let's eliminate one legislative chamber here and make the remaining one full-time, with outside job restrictions to discourage voting with personal interests or paychecks in mind.

Right now, donations come in during the legislature, that's very transparent, and while wrong, as the Honolulu Star-Advertiser editorialized last week, changing that fundraising rule would probably just force a change on the check date, but not the concept. Let's see if enough people, while in office, can stomach changes to make the public feel better about what goes on, and perhaps actually get interested, if legislators care. Think about it…

Is anybody out there? Does anybody care? Does being in office require accountability, or just friendly sign wavers every two years to ensure reelection?

Think about it.

May 21, 2018

Full Disclosure—Not!

Do you know how many really qualified, valuable people opt to not be part of important state boards and commissions? Neither do I; neither does anyone, as we'll never know who has opted out due to the unnecessarily restrictive disclosure rules that have been in place for four years. When the rules were made more stringent, at least 25 dedicated, unpaid people quit major boards, including the UH Board of Regents, the Land Use Commission, Land and Natural Resources, and the Hawaii Housing Finance and Development Corporation.

Well-meaning and ethical people don't mind a private ethics commission screening their finances, but making it available for the free world, as the rules now state, seems to be a bit over the top for volunteers. And that's our loss, as a community. When some of the best minds are sidelined by the legislature, the same people who trample all over ethics issues with their own self-serving votes, conflicts, and decisions, something is amiss.

The House deferred a bill to roll back the most stringent disclosure requirements in the session's final week. Those against relaxation point to less transparency, which could mean bad government, but is sharing one's entire family's finances with everyone really a fair and necessary alternative? Many thought this bill would pass, but it mysteriously died although both legislative bodies had similar bills moving ahead. And with its demise went 2018 hopes to bring more quality volunteers back into unpaid, vital, state boards and commissions. This oversight needs to be remedied without much thought in 2019. Legislators all have their outside jobs, yet vote on just about everything, without much second thought to conflicts. This is all so wrong. Think about it…

May 31, 2018

Issues Needing Answers

A few tidbits heading into your weekend… Signage at the Daniel K. Inouye International Airport in Honolulu will be temporarily covered up with placards as new gate and baggage claim signs evolve over time. Last week I went to drink out of a water fountain at this downtrodden facility so badly in need of repair, and no water came out. So I moved to the youth water fountain for height-challenged people next to it, and got sprayed in the eye with a gushing water flow. So the fact that there are signs that we'll see signs is surely a good start, but that's all it is. A billion-dollar renovation will hopefully do the trick at this traveler's house of horrors.

A few weeks back a hiker was rescued from the Haʻikū Stairway to Heaven. As we've discussed here ad nauseum over the past two decades—yes, decades—some entity needs to render a final decision on the fate of said stairs, before someone dies. Does that sound serious enough to warrant a resolution? Apparently not.

And finally, how numb have we become in this country? A recent headline said that the May 18 Texas high school shooting was the deadliest one since the Parkland, Florida, school shooting and that was way back in mid-February…of 2018. We are now reduced to counting school shooting time spans in months, if not weeks. Is this really the collateral damage we must expect in exchange for strict adherence to a 240-year-old document?

Can a modern-day, responsible, and ultimately productive discussion be held to address these horrific, too frequent occurrences? Or do we all go to our corners and just let time erode our faith and hope? Statistics say you are 17 times or 40 times more likely to be killed as a combat soldier than as a student. Really, so we're morally reduced to statistics comparing these vastly incongruent life positions in the same sentence—as if that might provide some assurance to bewildered parents and a befuddled populace? Talks and action on racial injustice and Me Too, but not this issue? Also, just how prepared are we locally to deal with this new, and sad, academic reality? Think about it…

Think about it..

June 18, 2018

Bet On It

Let the games begin! I'm not talking about soccer's World Cup or the start of NFL training camp, but rather the discussions that should be occurring today among legislators about whether Hawai'i should now jump on the sports betting bandwagon. Last month, the Supreme Court struck down sports betting laws that precluded individual states, outside of Nevada, from allowing legal sports gambling. Over 60 percent of American adults gambled over the past 12 months. Over 80 percent say that gambling is legitimate and casinos are okay. Gambling generates more revenue than movies, spectator sports, theme parks, cruise ships, and recorded music combined.

Now I am well aware of some of the inherit problems that gambling might bring, but let's face local reality. Many thousands illegally bet on sports here, and there are plenty more who fly to Vegas often to do the same. Since we're not going to soon allow shipboard gambling—even offshore—perhaps sports gambling is a way to reap much-needed benefits for all, including the hundreds of thousands here who don't bet on sports. We've all heard the tales about the illegal gambling underground—nagging debts, heavy-handed collections people, etc. And the fear of being found out no doubt precludes some betting abusers from handling their addiction issues. It's time to talk about local, legal sports gambling, controlled, and with targeted funding recipients.

It is estimated by the American Gaming Association that there is more than $150 billion wagered illegally on sporting events in the USA each year. Since Hawai'i's population represents four-tenths of one percent of the country's populace, simple math suggests there might be more than $590 million bet here yearly on sports. If just 20 percent of that money went toward education, repairing parks and sports fields, upgrading infrastructure, providing housing... the list goes on. So who will be the brave proponents right now, before the legislature convenes, to discuss this real opportunity as we await the 2019 legislative session. Let's listen to the arguments, because legalized local sports wagering might be a good bet for Hawai'i starting soon. Think about it…

Wanna bet there'll be repeated Las Vegas travel/casino lobbying efforts to quash any local sports gambling initiative in the Islands?

June 25, 2018

Seating Disorder

The Neal S. Blaisdell Center Master Plan has been created, morphed, discussed, revised, revamped, and is now moving toward execution. And it's a winner…mostly. If all goes according to plans, renovation work could begin in two years. The Terrace, the Civic Plaza, Coconut Grove, The Gardens, a new parking structure, pools of water, moving water, and other aesthetic enhancements will surely modernize this 54-year-old facility so badly in need of modernization.

But a big mistake is being made in the plans to simply upgrade the existing arena from approximately 6,500 seats to under 9,000 seats. That is plainly not enough additional seating to make it economically feasible for Honolulu to attract major concert attractions that currently aren't set up to play at a 50,000-seat outdoor Aloha Stadium nor able to work out the numbers to make two or three indoor shows work out. Simple math, we need a larger concert and sports venue. Then, major concert acts and professional sports events can play here for one night and earn their living, without promoters having to book two or three nights, which is currently the problem, as you then have to pay up to twice the rent, artist fees, security, etc.

Adding fewer than 2,500 seats to the Blaisdell Arena will not get the job done. Check out most of the major mainland concert venues where artists perform across the country, and you'll see that having at least 12,000 to 15,000 seats represents the sweet spot. One night, one show, event costs that work for the promoter, and ticket prices that should seem reasonable for fans. There have been public hearings, but perhaps it's still not too late, as interested stakeholders, like Live Nation, AEG, pro sports leagues, and others need to be consulted before we renovate an obsolete building by adding only 2,000 seats, and then find out that top acts and events still can't make the numbers work here. Think about it…

Oh, and then there's the estimated $720 million price tag for this project, from the same folks who brought you the $5 billion, er, $7 billion, er, $9 billion rail project. We need a 12,000- to 15,000-seat Blaisdell.

June 28, 2018

Teacher Tension

While not really surprising, it was still a reality check to learn a week ago that teachers are leaving Hawaiʻi at an astounding rate—up 84 percent in the past eight years. It simply costs too much for too many to consider staying or even coming here, and there are fewer people who see teaching as a career path for themselves when they attend college, perhaps in part because of the realities of the costs of living local.

And please, no more talk about $750,000 affordable condos or homes—for sale or for rent—that's simply not a reality for far too many people trying to make ends meet and have enough saved up to live out their golden years in Hawaiʻi, and that includes teachers. We talk about our keiki and the need to improve the test scores and value of an education here. Well, that goal gets tougher if we don't have enough qualified people to adequately teach with reasonable class sizes and long-term plans to stay here.

We've discussed concerns about a possible local brain drain as kids opt not to return home due to salary disparity and the cost of living here, and it appears that the future locally might not be too rosy for people who've earned higher degrees—not only doctors, but also teachers. And one can safely assume that other professions requiring higher education are feeling the sting of housing costs, salary realities, and other concerns far beyond traffic and the cost of a gallon of milk. The price one pays for living in paradise, the "paradise tax," may affect what paradise looks like in the coming decades; some solutions are needed soon. Think about it.

July 19, 2018

Rabid Transit

Two weeks ago, in case you missed it or have simply become numb to news about this project, we learned that the Honolulu rail project is apparently still short by $134 million. But hey, what's $134 million among friends? Frankly, at this point in time and when we're at more than double the original budget, $134 million sounds like a simple rounding error. Yes, that's how silly the numbers have gotten on this project.

And since we are still at least eight, yes eight, years away from the currently estimated completion of the entire project, does anyone really think we've seen the end of miscalculations on this financial sinkhole? The Feds thought the project seemed to be heading toward a $250 million shortfall way back in April. And now an independent firm seems to think the underpayment amount will actually be $134 million. This is not chump change, but it is also sadly not the last time fiscal fiddling will be done before the first train rolls down the tracks to Ala Moana Center.

You know the budget is pliable and flexible when the official paperwork is done in pencil and everyone is supplied an eraser before each meeting. Just kidding… How anybody can put an absolute cost figure on this project in mid-2018 is actually quite befuddling, knowing that there will be more obstacles in the way as the congested town area starts getting excavated in the coming eight years. We sadly say ho hum nowadays when the latest calculations come in. There's been nothing "rapid" about this so-called rapid transportation project thus far, except for the constant rhetoric and shallow reassurances that all is well. Think about it…

Great to see that things have worked out for all of this. Oh, wait…

July 2, 2018

Sham of a Farcical Mockery

Not a great week for state entities last week. First we got word that, according to a coworker, some of the kids who run things day-to-day at the state Emergency Management Agency were either watching TV, movies, or asleep while on the job at times. On the heels of a false nuclear alert, that's not good, right? While names were mostly redacted in the report shown to the media, it was surely Moe, Larry, or Curly who are guilty in this one, yeh? And the movie they watched was War Games, so perhaps that counts as training for false alerts.

And then we had yet another management change at the Hawaii Tourism Authority, with the CEO being let go. Yet it seems nowadays there is more of a request from some locals for fewer tourists rather than fewer management staff at HTA. Over the last four years, 11 HTA staffers have left or been asked to leave, which is an eye-opener, considering that HTA has just 30 employees total (when fully staffed), including contract workers. Oh, and the HTA-appointed chair, his term ended this past weekend, with no apparent political will to retain him from the governor and tourism-involved legislators. Heck, this is starting to sound like the horror film series The Purge, or, as we see it locally, it looks like just another year at the Honolulu City Council, where the deck chairs on that Titanic are rearranged just about every year or so.

In the meantime, we have record tourism numbers amid strife and political gamesmanship, with concerns about vacation rentals and too many ignorant guests overrunning our precious ecosystem, thanks in part to good old social media gone wild. Is it any wonder that people question authority, leadership, and the value of voting here? When far too often the people in charge—either elected people or volunteer helpers—simply can't seem to get along or do what appears necessary to make their organizations run right? Actually, voting is the best way to ensure that at least you have some say in what goes on and with whom. Not that the choices here in the voting booth are always optimal, but you do get to decide and make a difference. Think about it…

Think about it.

Water Wonder

Desalination has been a not-so-hot topic for many years locally. Australia, Singapore, and Israel make the concept work for their countries today. It can work. But turning seawater into potable water is something that sounds simpler than it really is, and it's historically cost far too much for private concerns and governments to make a go of it. And while the concept sounds cool, costs invariably squash uneconomical plans every time.

But a new project is taking shape at the University of Hawai'i Mānoa, as reported by Hawaii News Now last month. A $2 million grant from the US Department of Energy Solar Energy Technologies Office will hopefully show that there really is an economically feasible way to get drinking water from the ocean. The technical side of this—which involves using a different form of osmosis than has been traditionally used—is way beyond my scientifically challenged brain, but suffice to say, this new idea is progressive and provides a new way of thinking about salt water and large scale ways to extract drinkable and usable H2O from the sea.

Some question this specific technology, but do like the idea of moving forward. The Honolulu Board of Water Supply planned a desalination plant for Kapolei 15 years ago. That didn't come to fruition. But it's now 2018, and perhaps we are closer to tapping natural resources to make sure we have ample fresh water from various places in the decades ahead. Think about it...

August 2, 2018

Strange, but True

Some odds and ends to send you off into your weekend… Scientists from Europe believe they may have finally discovered a buried lake on Mars, which they believe will help in their understanding about Mars's beginnings, and the history of water—on Mars. In the meantime, wariness and weariness continue in Maui's water rights battle. Perhaps we can simplify that discourse by simply providing a PVC pipeline directly from Mars to the Valley Isle. Water rights here and elsewhere are becoming as sacred as oil rights have been for the past 50 years, so while the news from Mars is exciting to some, figuring out how to share and preserve life-sustaining water on this planet surely deserves more coverage and resolution, no offense to any Martians watching.

Speaking of Maui, a white unicorn was found floating off of Olowalu Beach in western Maui about two weeks ago, thus heightening the happiness of small children throughout the state who often wonder about going through life without ever seeing a sasquatch, a menehune, or the beloved, mythical unicorn. Yes, I know it was a plastic float they found off of Maui, but how did it get there? I'm sure we'll have a committee assess this ocean-going discovery soon, followed by public comments, a fact finding commission, and more commentary.

And finally, it's great to see the girders and pillars to handle the rapid transit tracks going up mauka of the highway just west of the airport. But since the actual usage of this train segment is three to five years away, can we at least get some Olympic luge or toboggan practice going when it's completed but not in use? Think about it…

Let's keep Mars in the fiction section of our to-do list for now, as we first try to ensure that we have better air to breathe on Earth in the coming decades.

Think about it

September 3, 2018

Streets of Nightmares

As we finally have seen some sunny days, with more to follow until the next threat from Mother Nature, the time has come to perhaps reassess priorities in how we our repaving our many dilapidated streets on Oʻahu. My quiet neighborhood had decent streets, yet they all got repaved a while back. A viewer who I've bumped into twice recently said that her neighborhood streets were also just fine, yet those side streets also got repaved. Hmmm... So why can't we seem to get things handled on Vineyard Boulevard, Ward Avenue, Kapiʻolani Boulevard, the horrid Pali Highway, Ala Moana Boulevard, Likelike Highway, Liliha Street, Waimānalo Road...? The list goes on and on; you know it in your neck of the woods, too. Nimitz Highway has been repaved more times than a fading Hollywood star, and many communities wince as they bear their major road breakdowns.

I don't know about roadway repair timing or city and state master plans, but with limited resources, you have to wonder why some neighborhood roads in seemingly decent shape are getting repaved well before the streets that thousands of cars unhappily bump along every day. I am sure there is a method to this seeming madness, but it's hard to fathom, week after week, as our tires, shocks and nerves are jiggled about by potholes, cracks, upraised sewers and metal plates, and just plain, consistent, poor overall upkeep.

And then there's the question about the actual material that is used locally. Stronger, more expensive repaving material, like cement, would lessen the incessant reparations needed often down the road on major roads. Concrete lasts longer and is much better than asphalt at handling heavy truck wear and tear. Vehicles use less gas on concrete roads, but concrete is more slippery than asphalt, and costs are obviously a big factor. I think. Bottom line, we all pay the price for bad roads, but perhaps a little more logic and timing can go into what roads are fixed when, and with what. Think about it...

Think about it.

Comfortably Numb

I read what I felt was an interesting article in my college alma mater's quarterly magazine recently. It was a piece written by the author of a new book called Bad Stories: What the Hell Just Happened to Our Country, and the lines that stuck with me quoted another author who stated 30 years ago that in our society nowadays serious debate, ideas and literature are now more likely to be compromised or marginalized than ever before. Book author Steve Almond then wrote, "The result was that every aspect of our culture (politics, religion, news) had been reduced to entertainment. Americans had devolved from an electorate into an audience."

Almond suggests that we have "…abandoned the duties of citizenship for the pleasures of fandom." More people than ever before devote more time to their favorite sports teams than they do to other pursuits—like politics, volunteer work, or even faith. And I wonder if the age-old apathy seen right here in Hawai'i nei is simply a byproduct of all of this. Yes, I know we have ostensibly a one-party system in Hawai'i, which allows the ruling class to not be pressured very often in fear of losing its jobs or status. But isn't this where an active, engaged citizenry must step forward and demand more? More answers, more help, more solutions, more vision?

After all, nowadays we have more, easier ways to communicate and to rally around issues and items of importance than ever before. As this election season evolves, take the time to let your voice be heard, rally your friends and neighbors on issues vital to you and your community, and make sure you vote. Let's not allow for further civic atrophy through disinterest as we risk becoming numb or acting helpless via redundancy of 24-hour cable news babble, overuse of cell phones, unsocial media, and quiet disengagement. Think about it…

Thinkabout it.

Road/House Blues

It's been five years since we heard about a hold up for a possible zipper lane to help ease traffic heading in the leeward direction in the afternoons. In the meantime, not much more has been said, or done. Yes, the costs were creeping up, that's why we heard about a delay, but since the original zipper lane is now 20 years old, you might have thought that a solution to provide the same traffic-abating service to people heading home to central and west Oʻahu would be in place now. No such luck, or apparent strategy, solution, or sense of urgency.

So, any day, including many weekends, you can plan to wait an extra 20 minutes to an hour getting from town to your westward destination as you fight traffic, frustration, and the setting sun. Why this project has taken so long with so little sense of resolution is baffling, until you look at so many other issues that sit out there, apparently beyond our political grasp. 20 years ago, we figured out how to get thousands of cars and people into town quicker during the daily rush hour commute...yet we just can't figure out how to get them back home quickly on the same road. Really?

The Nimitz contraflow lane is now 15 years old, so we really have seen multiple forms of government in action when it comes to getting people into town. But it's government inaction when it relates to quickening the plight of heading westward out of town, and, of course, as it relates to leeward side alternatives to Farrington Highway when it is backed up due to accidents or other problems. But hey, that discussion is only 25 years old or so, so we still have time. Just like the Stairway to Heaven and Waikīkī natatorium issues that seemingly linger forever, or at least multiple decades. Think about it...

A zipper lane heading ʻewa in the afternoon? Could it be? That's radical thinking—after all, we've had one town-bound in the mornings for about 20 years. We'll do a study on it and get right back to you.

Think about it.

December 3, 2018

What We've Lost...

Empathy. The ability to share or at least understand the feelings of others. A sense of soul. That's what we've lost as a country. That's what is readily missing day in and day out from our elected officials in Washington, DC. The rancor and need to be heard without listening. The mandate to meet supposed constituents' desires without even considering the other side. I'm not talking about pity or sympathy, I'm talking about simple points of view that others might have, that maybe you should consider, that perhaps might lead to solution and—God forbid—compromise. Empathy indicates emotional intelligence and shows a concern about the greater good.

We'll need some empathy here during the upcoming legislative session, no doubt. Even within a one-party system, there are huge divisions based on ego, selfishness, and the desire to ensure that those I didn't want don't get what they want, perhaps even if the people lose out. Watch it closely. Top-ranked chairs and party leaders who didn't back our current governor in the nasty primary election now have to work side by side to get things done. Forget the stultifying Senate and House rifts we'll see in DC in 2019 and 2020; keep an eye on the local posturing when major decision items come down in the 100-day legislative session this winter.

Can those elected and appointed put aside their differences for the common good? Can memories be short-term for the health of this state? Can people destroy their voodoo dolls and work proactively to move items forward to truly make a difference? Or will we see posturing, vetoes, and backroom death knells for ideas brought up by people we simply didn't want to be where they are—in positions of power. Empathy is a value we've buried, for now, as a country. Let's hope we can find some this upcoming legislative session. Think about it...

December 6, 2018

HTA and the Future

"Hawai'i is a place where people live—not just a place that they visit," so says the new Hawaii Tourism Authority head honcho, Chris Tatum. A Radford High School graduate and longtime veteran of the local hotel industry who got his start in housekeeping at the Royal Hawaiian Hotel as a teenager, Tatum has spent time running Neighbor Island Marriott properties and also has vast experience on the West Coast and in Asia. He seems to be the right person for the job among a hundred candidates that were vetted. We should all wish him well.

We are at a vital moment in time as travel and political leaders envision what the guest industry of the future in Hawai'i will look like and should look like. Many, if not most, local residents understand the huge value the visitor industry provides to our local economy. At the same time, many here express frustration about crowded places off the beaten path that are now being trod on, sometimes with little respect, by visitors. Of course, some locals fall into that "no respect" category too, but that's another story. We need vision.

Kailua is no longer a quaint village on weekends, as more people discover its charms via social media and good old word of mouth. There are a more bikes, pedestrians, and beach goers, alongside discovery-oriented visitors appearing daily from illegal vacation rentals. Hopefully, Mr. Tatum and the HTA staff can work alongside an often-surly legislature as they also listen to community voices, as we finish up yet another record-breaking year of visitors and visitor spending. Hawai'i's charm is a major reason guests keep coming, and that needs to be protected above all else in planning the tourism road in the decades ahead. If you build it, they will come. But you better preserve "it"—the many intangible assets that make Hawai'i such a special place. Think about it…

Prison Wisdom

A guy walks out of a prison… Sounds like the beginning of a joke. Well, what transpired after this local and true story is a joke, but it's not funny. Yet no individuals are apparently to blame. No one is going to feel further consequences. It took eight hours before the state hospital even called 911 to report that this murderer was missing, but no one is at fault. He had two fake IDs and about $6,000 in cash, got into a cab, got on a plane, and left town. And no one is at fault. At least that's the ultimate conclusion—this incident simply happened. Institutional failure, perhaps. Human lethargy, inattentiveness, or misconduct? Nah…

The accused had also apparently engaged in past sexual relations with staff, he unlocked a combination lock during his escape, and he'd received contraband in the past. Ho hum. Granted, the Hawaii State Hospital is a treatment center, not a prison, but that doesn't mean some of the inmates are any less dangerous than those locked behind bars elsewhere. So the fault lies in the system. And just like oftentimes when other things fail at state or city levels, we never go through the difficult, but necessary, procedures to assess responsibility on humans, to make people accountable, to ensure absolute understanding of roles…it's always the system.

Like last January's false missile alert, the driver's license and ID cards snafu this year, the now biannual election office issues—always system failures. Like the 8,000 plus unauthorized vacation rentals that go unchecked, the system is simply overwhelmed. The list goes on and on. When systems fail, there is often an obvious lack of human accountability. But we don't like shame people. Granted, some procedures have changed at the state hospital since the murderer escaped, and that's good. But are we always so afraid of legal repercussions that we rarely deal with the human component when blatant errors occur? How drastic a mistake has to be made before simple job accountability and responsibility comes into play? Think about it…

Think about it.

January 7, 2019

Of Council

The Honolulu City Council has finally resolved its seemingly annual leadership struggles by beginning 2019 with a new dilemma—no leadership. No committee assignments have been made yet, so no one can get tossed yet from a chairmanship position on any committee. But this hardly counts as progress. It is actually the result of seven weeks of waiting for the filing of and subsequent decision on a challenge to the election of presumed chair-to-be Trevor Ozawa, who seemed to have won his seat by a mere 22 votes back on November 6.

Ah, but nothing is what it seems to be when it comes to the often-bickering city council, but this misadventure is actually not the fault of internal positioning, egos, or political posturing by mayoral wannabes. The system (ah, that lovely word used far too often when things go wrong in officialdom here) seems to have failed in the voting process, and it has taken more than seven weeks for a to-be-announced decision to be rendered. So Ozawa sat by on the opening day of January 2, drank the ceremonial 'awa with his council brethren in a half in, half out polka, and now waits to see what's next. Well, at least he got a little buzz out of the drawn out, first day, no chair announcement proceedings while sighing in obvious frustration.

We now await a state supreme court decision about what happens next with an updated ruling on the election verdict veracity question in Council District 4—a recount, litigation, hanging chads, who knows? One thing that won't happen just yet is business as usual in the Honolulu City Council's chambers. Which means we'll have to wait longer than usual for the inevitable, but not mandatory, reshuffling of hierarchy positions as egos fray over the coming months. But maybe not. Maybe 'awa can be served regularly with some 1970s Tangerine Dream music wafting in the background to help ease nerves and let business get done in a collegial, cooperative manner. Once we get started, that is… Think about it.

Never overestimate the underwhelming capacity of the Honolulu City Council to get along and get things done, sans drama.

Think about it…

January 14, 2019

Of Change

And thus, we head into the home stretch. KFVE will be undergoing some backroom changes. You, the viewers, will be able to enjoy the station just as you have for the past 30 years, since its inception. But I will be moving on. Ownership; industry; FCC; and Washington, DC; changes mean that my position will be eliminated at the end of next week. It has been a complete pleasure to be at the helm here at KFVE and before that, at KHNL, too, for many, many years. I have enjoyed sharing thoughts with you, as well as some incredible programming, from UH sports for 28 years to our award-winning local news to vital local programming, such as the Merrie Monarch Festival, weekly local programs, and much, much more. But times change.

These editorials, these simple, twice a week 90-second vignettes aired within our news have been running on-air and in your house, when you've allowed it, for over 19 years now. Feel old? I have written and, with the incredible help of our wonderful team here at Hawaii News Now, produced and aired over 1,980 editorials during this two-decade window. And yes, I have written every one of these "Think About It..." editorials myself, even when sidelined with surgeries or when out of town on vacation or business—I simply recorded a few extra editorials to make up for my absence. That was my vow—to be here twice weekly every week, no matter what.

These editorials have always come from my head and my heart, with a conscious and sincere effort to try to make a little difference to someone or something along the way. If that seems arrogant, I'm sorry, but when given a powerful platform, I believe people should try to make things better. I believe in the incredible power of local broadcast; I have been a part of it here in Hawai'i for over 40 years now, and we'll see where that focus and belief system takes me next. I could not have been done these segments without the help from statistics, events, people, insanity, and suggestions from all over the place. I have tried, for the most part, to keep these thoughts relevant to local issues, needs, concerns, people, opportunities, and celebrations, with an occasional philanthropic or philosophical thought thrown in, too. I have appreciated your feedback, well, most of it, and I look forward to finishing up strong during my short time remaining here at KFVE. As always, think about it...

Think about it.

A Difference

Along with a number of nice texts and emails I received last week after announcing my retirement from KFVE at the end of this week, I got a lovely handwritten note from Sylvia, who said, "You did a job you loved and it showed." I can't think of a nicer thing for someone to say, as it relates to your work life. Who we are and what we do are two very different things. But who we are surely comes through in what we do. While you might be identified by your day-to-day job, the way you treat people and the way you try to make a difference in the lives of those around you will hopefully last far beyond your work years. Leave a legacy of love, if you will…

In the book The Carpenter, author Jon Gordon regales the value of three things that make all the difference: loving, serving, and caring. We should all strive to do these things in profound ways on a regular basis, as best we can. We should all endeavor to live with passion, and please, avoid drama at every turn. It is destructive, counter-productive, and the physical and mental weight of drama is something to avoid as often as possible. But doing right, doing what you love, whether as a teacher, parent, legislator, coach, waiter, TSA agent, friend, relative—that's what we've got to give while we are here. When you're in charge, are you a manager or a leader and mentor? When you give or connect, is it sincere and with empathy, or is it about what's in it for me?

If nothing else over these past 19 years of editorializing, I've tried to say something that might make a difference, because I truly believe we live in the greatest place on earth with the opportunity to take our east meets west meets Polynesia melting pot and show the world. Yes, we're human, imperfect, but coachable, and we should all do our best every day to focus on what matters and who matters in our lives. As that vaunted philosopher Yoda once said, "Do or do not, there is no try." I encourage you to keep doing. Think about it…

Think about it..

January 24, 2019

Over and Out

I leave you tonight with this final editorial. Two of the things that always help me get through the tough times and the good times are humor and music. Try 'em out, and hopefully you'll see how laughing and singing can change your world at times. I leave you with some simple thoughts that resonate with me time after time:

All we are is dust in the wind (Kansas). It is amazing what you can accomplish if you do not care who gets the credit (Harry Truman). Rust never sleeps (Neil Young). I am not in this world to live up to your expectations, and you are not in this world to live up to mine. You are you, and I am I, and if by chance we find each other, it's beautiful. If not, it can't be helped (Fritz Perls). Just do it (Nike). We're living in an age where limitations are forgotten; the outer edges move and dazzle us, but the core is something rotten; and we're standing on the precipice of prejudice and fear; We trust science just as long as it tells us what we want to hear (Drive-By Truckers). Money, so they say, is the root of all evil today; but if you ask for a raise it's no surprise that they're giving none away (Pink Floyd). Do the right thing (Spike Lee). Happiness depends upon ourselves (Aristotle). When words fail, music speaks (William Shakespeare). Broken crayons still color (Shelley Hitz). Be yourself; everyone else is already taken (Oscar Wilde). I'm older now, but still running against the wind (Bob Seger). And please, keep watching KFVE for many, many more years (John Fink).

I could go on for hours with lyrics and lines and jokes that stimulate, relax, or excite the brain—well, my brain at least—but that would mess up our news and other programming. The bottom line is just do what's right, make a difference, look up from your dang phone and be in the real world, don't veer right when about to turn left, live aloha, and do question authority. I wish you the best in everything you do, and I thank you for sharing your valuable time with me and KFVE right here over these past 19 years. Aloha, and think about it…

Think about it.

Afterword

So there you have it—a veritable potpourri of commentary, selections from the "Think About It" editorial library over two decades in the life of a community. Perhaps you read this tome at the leisurely pace of one a day for six months. Perhaps you binge-read (what a concept!) over a short window of time. Perhaps you just got bored and skipped to the end. Or perhaps you're already looking forward to Volume 2!

There's no tidy summation or conclusion to this book, just a hope that everything is "to be continued," as we endeavor to right the wrongs, change what needs to be changed, better understand the universe we inhabit, recognize those deserving of acknowledgment, live with empathy and passion, and leave this mortal coil in better shape than we found it as we forge ahead, make a difference, and think about it...

Mahalo!

Think about it.

About the Author

John Fink is a business consultant, media specialist, writer and speaker who has spent 43 years in Hawaiʻi media, including 37 years in Honolulu television. Through his company, Think About It, LLC, he provides business seminars for management teams and employees at various levels and does public speaking on "making a difference in life." He is also an emcee at numerous annual functions and plans to disc jockey at dance parties.

John was born in Long Island, New York, grew up in Highland Park, Illinois, and graduated from Wesleyan University in Middletown, Connecticut. Midway through his college career, he spent a semester attending the University of Hawaiʻi at Mānoa. He has been an integral part of Hawaiʻi's business, social, media, sports, entertainment, and philanthropic communities for more than four decades. He serves on a number of philanthropic boards and committees, including the Stadium Authority (Aloha Stadium), St. Francis Healthcare System, Big Brothers/Big Sisters Foundation, the Aloha Festival, Easterseals Hawaii's annual golf fundraiser, the Hawaii State Junior Golf Association, ʻAhahui Koa Ānuenue (UH athletics booster club), the Hawaiʻi Council on Economic Education, the Diamond Head Classic basketball tournament and the Hawaiʻi Bowl.

His website can be found at www.thinkaboutithawaii.com and he can be reached at john@thinkaboutithawaii.com.

Think about it.